Parallel Curriculum Units for Mathematics

Grades 6–12

Parallel Curriculum Units for Mathematics

for

Mathematics

Grades 6–12

Jann H. Leppien | Jeanne H. Purcell

EDITORS

CORWIN

A SAGE Company

CORWIN
A SAGE Company

FOR INFORMATION:

Corwin
A SAGE Company
2455 Teller Road
Thousand Oaks, California 91320
(800) 233-9936
Fax: (800) 417-2466
www.corwin.com

SAGE Ltd.
1 Oliver's Yard
55 City Road
London EC1Y 1SP
United Kingdom

SAGE Pvt. Ltd.
B 1/I 1 Mohan Cooperative Industrial Area
Mathura Road, New Delhi 110 044
India

SAGE Asia-Pacific Pte. Ltd.
33 Pekin Street #02-01
Far East Square
Singapore 048763

Acquisitions Editor: Jessica Allan
Associate Editor: Allison Scott
Editorial Assistant: Lisa Whitney
Production Editor: Melanie Birdsall
Copy Editor: Alison Hope
Typesetter: C&M Digitals (P) Ltd.
Proofreader: Cheryl Rivard
Indexer: Sheila Bodell
Cover Designer: Rose Storey
Permissions Editor: Karen Ehrmann

Copyright © 2011 by Corwin

Printed in the United States of America

Library of Congress Cataloging-in-Publication Data

Parallel curriculum units for mathematics, grades 6–12 / editors, Jann H. Leppien, Jeanne H. Purcell.

p. cm.
Includes bibliographical references and index.

ISBN 978-1-4129-6548-4 (pbk.)

1. Mathematics—Study and teaching (Middle school)
2. Mathematics—Study and teaching (Secondary)
3. Curriculum planning. 4. Curriculum evaluation.
I. Leppien, Jann H. II. Purcell, Jeanne H. III. Title.

QA11.2.P366 2011   510.71'2—dc22   2010051777

This book is printed on acid-free paper.

11 12 13 14 15 10 9 8 7 6 5 4 3 2 1

Contents

Additional materials and resources related to
Parallel Curriculum Units for Mathematics, Grades 6–12
can be found at www.corwin.com/math6–12

List of Resources

The following Resources can be found at the companion website for *Parallel Curriculum Units for Mathematics, Grades 6–12* at www.corwin.com/math6–12.

About the Editors

Jann H. Leppien served as a coordinator of gifted and talented education in Montana prior to attending the University of Connecticut, where she earned her doctorate in gifted education and worked as a research assistant at the National Research Center for the Gifted and Talented. She has been a teacher for 33 years, spending 14 of those years working as a classroom teacher, enrichment specialist, and coordinator of the Schoolwide Enrichment Model in Montana. She is past president of the Montana Association for Gifted and Talented Education. Currently, she is an associate professor in the School of Education at the University of Great Falls in Montana. She teaches graduate and undergraduate courses in gifted education, educational research, curriculum and assessment, creativity, and methods courses in math, science, and social studies. Her research interests include teacher collaboration, curriculum design, underachievement, and planning instruction for advanced learners. She works as a consultant to teachers in the field of gifted education and as a national trainer for the Talents Unlimited Program. She is coauthor of *The Multiple Menu Model: A Parallel Guide for Developing Differentiated Curriculum.* She is active in the National Association for Gifted Children (NAGC), serving as a board member, and is a board member of the Association for the Education of Gifted Underachieving Students.

Jeanne H. Purcell is the consultant to the Connecticut State Department of Education for gifted and talented education. She is also director of UConn Mentor Connection, a nationally recognized summer mentorship program for talented teenagers that is part of the NEAG Center for Talent Development at the University of Connecticut. Prior to her work at the State Department of Connecticut, she was an administrator for Rocky Hill Public Schools (Connecticut); a program specialist with the National Research Center on the Gifted and Talented, where she worked collaboratively with other researchers on national issues related to high-achieving young people; an instructor of Teaching the Talented, a graduate-level program in gifted education; and a staff developer to school districts across this country and in Canada. She has been an English teacher, community service coordinator, and teacher of the gifted, K–12, for 18 years in Connecticut school districts. She has published many articles that have appeared in *Educational Leadership, Gifted Child Quarterly, Roeper Review, Educational and Psychological Measurement, National Association of Secondary School Principals' Bulletin, Our Children: The National PTA Magazine, Parenting for High Potential,* and *Journal for the Education of the Gifted.* She is active in the National Association for Gifted Children (NAGC); she serves on the awards committee and the curriculum committee of NAGC, for which she is the co-chair for the annual Curriculum Awards Competition.

About the Contributors

Marianne Cavanaugh has 32 years of classroom experience at the middle and high school levels. She has been an adjunct professor of Calculus 1 and Honors Calculus at the University of Connecticut since 1998, and is currently the University Academic Specialist for Calculus 1. She is the 1998 Presidential Award Winner for Excellence in Mathematics and Science Teaching and is the 1998 Connecticut Teacher of the Year. She has presented math workshops at the national (NCTM), state, and local levels, and has presented at the AP Conference in topics ranging from problem solving and the appropriate use of technology, to differentiated and scaffolded mathematics instruction at the middle school, high school, and college levels. She is a trainer for Data-Driven Decision Making/Data Teams, Common Formative Assessments, and Effective Teaching Strategies, and is a Level 3 mathematics trainer for Laying the Foundation. Marianne is currently the Connecticut National Math and Science Initiative (NMSI) Math Content Director for AP Calculus, AP Statisitics, and AP Java for Project Opening Doors.

Amy J. Germundson is a graduate research assistant and doctoral student at the University of Virginia. She is currently a PhD candidate in Curriculum and Instruction with an emphasis in STEM fields. Previously, she taught a variety of high school mathematics and physical science courses, as well as seventh-grade science in the International Baccalaureate program. While teaching, Amy earned an MEd in Science Curriculum and Instruction and Space Science. She has a passion for working with teachers both nationally and internationally on authentic curriculum and assessment design, concept-based learning, and ways to inspire and reach diverse learners in STEM fields.

Carrie Heaney is currently the mathematics department coordinator and an eighth-grade mathematics teacher at Sky Vista Middle School in Aurora, Colorado. Carrie has been a mathematics educator for the past 12 years. She is the 2009 Recipient of the Presidential Award for Excellence in Mathematics and Science Teaching and the 2007 Colorado Council of Teachers of Mathematics, Outstanding Teacher Award. In addition to teaching eighth grade and working with the teachers in her building, Carrie also supports mathematics teachers in the Cherry Creek School District by leading classes on implementing the district's mathematics curriculum as well as classes on understanding how students develop numeracy and the effect that has on a student's understanding of multiplication, division, and place value.

Helen Weingart started her career in education in 1967. She has taught Grades 4–12 and currently works as a staff development specialist at EASTCONN, a Regional Education Service Center in northeastern Connecticut. For the past 22 years, she has facilitated mathematics workshops and projects and has provided training on a range of instructional strategies and curriculum development topics. She worked with the Connecticut State Department of Education and mathematics teacher experts from across the state to create a comprehensive mathematics curriculum, which included a performance assessment component, "Goals 2000 Mathematics Curriculum." She currently is the Field Operations Project Manager for Project Opening Doors, a National Math and Science Initiative Advanced Placement grant awarded to Connecticut that focuses on providing opportunities for underserved student populations to participate in math, science, and English AP courses.

Introduction to the Parallel Curriculum Model

When *The Parallel Curriculum: A Design to Develop High Potential and Challenge High-Ability Learners* was published (Tomlinson et al., 2002), the six of us who wrote the work knew we had found ideas in the model to be interesting, challenging, and worthy of more thought and articulation. Since the original book's publication more than six years ago, we have spent a great deal of time talking among ourselves and with other practitioners about the Parallel Curriculum Model (PCM). These colleagues were as passionate as we were about the nature of high-quality curriculum and the increasing need for such learning experiences for all students. Our colleagues offered us invaluable viewpoints, opinions, suggestions, and probing questions. We surely benefitted in countless ways from their expertise and insights.

Our conversations led to the publication of two additional books about PCM in 2006: *Book I, The Parallel Curriculum in the Classroom: Essays for Application Across the Content Areas, K–12*, featured articles that we hope clarified and expanded on selected aspects of the model. We continue to hope that it helps educators think more deeply about important facets of the model and some of its "nonnegotiable" components. *Book II, The Parallel Curriculum in the Classroom: Units for Application Across the Content Areas, K–12*, invited readers to consider eight curriculum units that were designed using PCM. As we compiled the units, we sought to answer the question, "What is necessary in the design process of any PCM unit?"

We did not consider these units as off-the-shelf selections that a teacher might pick up and teach. Rather, we viewed the eight units as professional development tools helpful to any educator who wanted to reflect on one way of creating thoughtful curriculum.

Over the past two years, we have continued to engage in conversations about the nature of curriculum models and how they can be used to create rigorous learning opportunities for students. As before, these conversations ultimately led us to two additional projects. The first was to create an updated version of the original publication. This second edition of PCM was completed in spring 2008 and is titled *The Parallel Curriculum: A Design to Develop Leaner Potential and Challenge Advanced Learners* (Tomlinson et al., 2008). The second edition of the PCM extends our understanding of how this framework for curriculum development can be used to create, revise, or adapt curricula to the needs of all students. In addition, it explores the concept of ascending levels of intellectual demand for all learners in today's heterogeneous classrooms.

The second project was the creation of a series of curriculum units, based on PCM, that could be used by practitioners. To address the varying needs of teachers across the K–12 grade span—as well as across different content areas—we decided to create a series of five publications. The first publication is dedicated to the elementary grades, K–5. It features lessons and curriculum units that have been designed to address the needs of primary and elementary learners.

The last four publications span the secondary grades, Grades 6–12. Each of the four publications focuses on a different content area: English/Language Arts, Social Studies/History, Science, and Mathematics. It is our hope that the lessons in each not only underscore important and discipline-specific content, but also illuminate the four parallels in unique and enduring ways.

We could not have completed these tasks without the invaluable assistance of two new team members. Cindy Strickland contributed to both publications in 2006, and also created the "Parallel Curriculum Multimedia Kit." Marcia Imbeau is also a longtime user and trainer in PCM; she edited the K–5 book in this series.

THE PARALLEL CURRICULUM MODEL: A BRIEF OVERVIEW

There is a wonderfully illuminating fable from India about seven blind men who encounter an elephant. Because each man felt a different part of the beast with his exploring hands, none was able to figure out the true nature of the gigantic creature. They realized, then, "Knowing in part may make a fine tale, but wisdom comes from seeing the whole" (Young, 1992).

Did you ever stop to think that students' perceptions about their learning experiences might be as limited as the perceptions the blind men had about the nature of the elephant? Perhaps, like the blind men, students learn only bits and pieces of the curriculum over time, never seeing, let alone understanding, the larger whole that is humankind's accumulated knowledge.

What if we were able to design curriculum in a multifaceted way to ensure that all learners understand (1) the nature of knowledge, (2) the connections that link humankind's knowledge, (3) the methodology of the practitioner who creates knowledge, and (4) the "fit" between the learner's values and goals and those that characterize practicing professionals? How would classrooms be different if the focus of curriculum was qualitatively differentiated curriculum that prompts learners not only to accumulate information, but also to experience the power of knowledge and their potential role within it?

The PCM suggests that all learners should have the opportunity to experience the elephant and benefit from "seeing the whole." Moreover, as students become more expert in their understanding of all the facets of knowledge, the curriculum should support students' developing expertise through ascending levels of intellectual demand. This overview of PCM will provide readers with a very brief summary of the model and an opportunity to see how the sum of the model's component parts can be used to create qualitatively differentiated curriculum for *all* students.

THE PARALLEL CURRICULUM: A UNIQUE CURRICULUM MODEL

What is a curriculum model? Why are there so many models from which to choose? A curriculum model is a format for curriculum design developed to meet unique needs, contexts, goals, and purposes. To address specific goals and purposes, curriculum developers design or reconfigure one or more curriculum components (see Figure I.1) to create their models. The PCM is unique because it is a set of four interrelated yet parallel designs for organizing curriculum: Core, Connections, Practice, and Identity.

Figure I.1   Key Curriculum Components

Curriculum Component	Definition
Content	The knowledge, essential understandings, and skills students are to acquire
Assessment	Tools used to determine the extent to which students have acquired the content
Introduction	A precursor or foreword to a lesson or unit
Teaching Methods	Methods teachers use to introduce, explain, model, guide, or assess learning
Learning Activities	Cognitive experiences that help students acquire, rehearse, store, transfer, and apply new knowledge and skills
Grouping Strategies	The arrangement of students
Resources	Materials that support learning and teaching
Products	Performances or work samples that constitute evidence of student learning
Extension Activities	Enrichment experiences that emerge from representative topics and students' interests
Differentiation Based on Learner Need, Including Ascending Levels of Intellectual Demand	Curriculum modifications that attend to students' need for escalating levels of knowledge, skills, and understanding
Lesson and Unit Closure	Reflection on the lesson to ensure that the point of the learning experience was achieved or a connection to the unit's learning goal was made

THE FOUR CURRICULUM PARALLELS

Let's look at these parallel designs through the eyes of Lydia Janis, a fifth-grade teacher, who develops expertise in using the four parallels over several years. We will focus on one curriculum unit, Lydia's Civil War unit, in order to illuminate how it changes, or transforms, to accommodate the goals and purposes of each parallel. For the sake of our discussion, we will treat each parallel as a separate unit. In reality, teachers use the parallels fluidly to address students' talent development needs. At the end of this summary, we will speak directly to when and how these parallels are used. Readers wishing a more detailed analysis of Lydia's work are referred to Chapters 4 through 7 in both editions of *The Parallel Curriculum Model*.

The Core Curriculum

Lydia Janis sat at her kitchen table and looked over her textbook objectives and state frameworks for the Civil War unit. She was troubled. She realized that the textbook objectives were low level: they simply called for students to identify and describe facts, such as "Describe how the Civil War began," and "Identify the differences between the North and South." Her frameworks, on the other hand, required different kinds of knowledge and understandings: "Explain reasons for conflicts and the ways conflicts have been resolved in history" and "Understand causal factors and appreciate change over time."

Lydia realized that the content embedded in her frameworks—concepts and principles—lay at the heart of history as a discipline. These key understandings were vastly more powerful, enduring, and essential to the discipline than the facts in the textbook objectives. She decided to keep her textbook and use it as a resource, however. After all, the information was right there on her shelf, she was familiar with the contents, and the topics covered were fairly well aligned with her state frameworks. But Lydia decided to replace the more simplistic objectives found in the text with the objectives found in the state frameworks.

Lydia realized that the change in **content** would necessitate changes in other curriculum components. Her **assessments** would need to match the content. Her assessment tools would need to measure both pre- and post-assessment of students' conceptual understanding in addition to basic facts about the historical period. Her **introduction** would need to be retooled to prepare students for the various roles they would assume during the unit as analyzers of documents, data, maps, and events, and to lead them to the powerful understandings she had targeted.

Lydia's **teaching methods** would no longer be strictly didactic, such as lecture and direct instruction, but more inductive to support students as they constructed their own understanding of the period. Her **learning activities** invited students to think about and draw conclusions about maps, documents, and related data. She supplemented the textbook with other **resources**, such as primary source documents, college textbooks, and the PBS video series by Ken Burns, *The Civil War* (1990). She imagined that she would have students who wanted to pursue **extension activities**. She gathered a few books about the Underground Railroad, Abraham Lincoln, and strategic battles. Finally, because she knew that her students were at different stages in their ability to understand materials and content, she gathered print materials that varied in complexity from song lyrics and easy-to-decipher documents to several "dense" primary source documents so that all students could work at **ascending levels of intellectual demand**.

Lydia also altered the **products** that students created. In a variety of **grouping** arrangements, they completed document analysis worksheets, ongoing concept maps, and timelines to chronicle their deepening understandings about conflict and the causal relationships of events that led to the Civil War.

Lydia reflected on her work. She had made significant changes to her teaching and student learning, and she was confident in her improvements. She felt the power of the Core Curriculum as a foundational curriculum.

The Curriculum of Connections

Later in Lydia's career, she became aware of initiatives for interdisciplinary teaching. She was puzzled by some of the units that were labeled "interdisciplinary." A unit on Mexico, completed recently by fourth graders, came to mind. Students learned and performed the Mexican Hat Dance, held a fiesta during which they broke a piñata and ate tacos, viewed a display of Mexican money, and drew maps of the migration route of monarch butterflies. "Yikes," she thought. "This unit is an illusion. It *looks* integrated, but it lacks a powerful theme to tie the activities together."

Lydia sat looking at the Core Curriculum unit on the Civil War that she had created a few years ago. She thought about the concept that had focused her earlier work: conflict. It reminded her that history repeats itself across people, periods, and cultures: the Vietnam War, women's suffrage, the Civil Rights movement, and the civil war in Bosnia. This principle, "history repeats itself," held so much power. She realized that she could use the macroconcept, conflict, and the generalization, "history repeats itself," as the content centerpiece to help students build authentic and powerful "bridges" between their understanding of the American Civil War and other times, events, cultures, and people.

Lydia made preliminary plans for her Curriculum of Connections unit. She prepared some assessment prompts, with accompanying rubrics, to assess students' understanding of conflict and the idea that "history repeats itself." She developed a pre-assessment and essential questions for the introduction to clarify the focus for this unit: "What is a war? Do all conflicts have a resolution? Does history repeat itself?" She knew that her teaching strategies would need to help students make their own "bridges" for the connections between the American Civil war and other events and periods. She decided to emphasize synectics, metaphorical thinking, Socratic questioning, problem-based learning, and debriefing. Her learning activities emphasized analytic thinking skills to help students in the comparisons and contrasts they needed to make analogies. Her supplemental resources were more varied and covered more events, cultures, and periods than the resources she had used in her old Core unit; the materials that she developed to scaffold student thinking included many more graphic organizers, such as Venn diagrams and reader response questions. She was pleased when she realized that the products, grouping strategies, and extension activities would remain similar to those she had used in the Core Curriculum.

For students needing support with this unit, she developed more-detailed graphic organizers; for those needing increasing levels of ascending levels of intellectual demand, she thought of several unfamiliar contexts to which students could apply their new learning, such as the conflict between Northern Ireland and Ireland, and additional revolutionaries like Nelson Mandela and Elizabeth Cady Stanton. She tucked away these ideas for later use.

Lydia reflected on the modifications she had made. "This unit will benefit all my students, especially my abstract thinkers, students who value the 'big picture,' and my scholars," she thought. "It holds so much promise . . . it is much different from the Mexican Hat Dance unit."

The Curriculum of Practice

That summer, Lydia realized she could polish the same unit even more. Even though she had seen her students engaged and learning deeply about the Civil War, she began thinking more about how talent develops, specifically how students become acquainted with and skillful in the use of methodologies. "Now that students have the important ideas within and across disciplines, they need to learn how to act like practitioners," she thought.

So began Lydia's journey through the Curriculum of Practice. She sought out her state and national frameworks to identify the standards related to the role of the historian. To address them, she decided to invite students to read historical novels set during the mid-1800s and record the characters' feelings, images, and perspectives, as well as to note how the characters' behaviors changed throughout the story. Second, she would deepen students' understandings of these historical perspectives by asking them to read related primary source documents and find evidence to support the characters' feelings and attitudes.

In order for students to complete these tasks, she decided to focus her teaching on the skills of the historian: the steps of historical research, taking notes, determining bias, and analyzing point of view, to name a few. She decided to demonstrate or model these skills for students and then use more-indirect teaching methods, such as Socratic questioning, to help students construct their own analyses of primary source material. To help students focus on the methodology of the field, she decided to invite a local museum curator to take part in the introduction of the unit.

Lydia subsequently decided to scaffold students' work with a learning contract. The learning contract required specific learning activities and also asked students to complete several short-term products as well as a culminating project, which was their historical research. Lydia provided them with a rubric to guide and assess their final work. Lydia knew her grouping formats needed to be fluid to honor students' interests and acknowledge that there were times when students needed to work alone or in pairs. This fluidity would be especially important if students elected to complete extension activities around self-selected research questions.

To accommodate students with sophisticated knowledge about the historical research process, Lydia prepared a list of more-complex research topics that required ascending levels of intellectual demand, such as inviting advancing students to conduct oral histories on a topic of their choice.

Lydia reviewed the lessons that now reflected the Curriculum of Practice. "Wow," she thought. "So far, I have three ways to optimize learning." Lydia compared and contrasted the three sets of revisions to the Civil War unit: Core, Connections, and Practice. "Each approach is unique and powerful." And she understood why teaching artful curriculum was a satisfying, career-long journey. "What will I discover next?" she wondered.

The Curriculum of Identity

It was a student who set Lydia on her next journey through the PCM. His name was Jacob, and he had an amazing knowledge of American history. She envisioned this boy as a history professor, immersed in his own research about historical topics and mentoring others as they investigated questions not yet answered.

She spent time thinking about how she could "morph" her curriculum once more. The content for any Identity unit has a triple focus: her already rich Core curriculum; the ideas, attitudes, beliefs, dispositions, and life outlooks of a professional; and the learning profile of each student, including the student's interests, learning style preferences, values, and goals. Her task, she thought, would be to increase students' awareness about the degree of "fit" between their own emerging sense of self and the profile of practitioners in the field.

Lydia developed a survey of her students' abilities, interests, grouping preferences, goals, and co-curricular activities. Next, she sketched out the stages that students might go through as they went from an early awareness of and interest in history to self-actualization *through* the discipline. "This tool will help me identify where each student currently is on this continuum so I can support his or her progress," she thought.

Now familiar with the many teaching strategies available, Lydia selected visualization as an important method because students would have to move back and forth between their past self, current self, and future self. She also knew that she would use problem-based learning, simulations, and coaching to help students come to understand their place in the Civil War unit as they acted as historians, authors of historical fiction, or war correspondents.

She envisioned her students in varied grouping formats as they spent time with learning activities that required self-analysis and reflection, prediction, and goal setting, among other activities. Ideas for products came easily to Lydia: completed learning profiles, prompts that asked students to reflect on and note patterns in their changing profiles, and prompts that invited students to reflect on the fit between themselves and those of the guest speakers (such as a local historian and journalist) who would take part in the introduction to the unit.

Lydia anticipated several extension activities, including explorations about notable leaders from the 1860s, as well as less-well-known figures, such as the young women who dressed and fought as soldiers during the Civil War. As she gathered resources to support this unit and its potential extensions, she made sure that her collection featured a variety of introspective materials that would help students understand the beliefs, values, goals, achievements, and sacrifices made by practitioners and enable students' comparisons between their own emerging beliefs and attitudes and those of the professionals.

Lydia reflected on her continuing journey with the PCM, which elicited a clarity that comes only with time and persistence. She now understood deeply the model's power and promise. It held the power to awaken and support a teacher's passion and focused creativity. Equally important, it held great promise for uncovering and supporting the gifts and talents of *all* students.

Lydia imagined each of her students as a diamond (see Figure I.2). The model's four parallels—Core, Connections, Practice, and Identity—served as unique polishing tools to reveal the brilliance in each young person. The Core fostered deep understanding in a discipline, while Connections elicited the metaphoric thinking required to span the breadth of human knowledge. Practice advanced the methodological skills required to contribute in a field, and Identity cultivated the attitudes, values, and life outlook that are prerequisites to self-actualization in a field.

Figure I.2 Lydia's View of the PCM

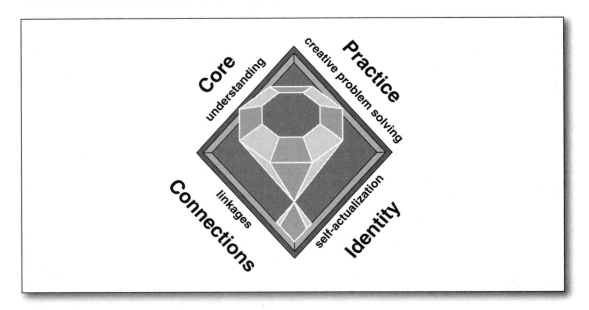

THE FOUR PARALLELS: WHEN AND HOW

We began this overview by talking about seven blind men, their limited perceptions about an elephant, and their ultimate realization, "Knowing in part may make a fine tale, but wisdom comes from seeing the whole." Lydia's work with each of the parallels illustrates how different curriculum components can be modified to help students gain an understanding and appreciation for the whole of a particular discipline.

There are an infinite number of ways to draw on the parallels. They can be used to revise or design tasks, lessons, or units. With a revised or designed unit "in hand," a teacher can move back and forth across one, some, or all parallels in a single unit. Equally attractive, a teacher might use just one parallel to extend a Core unit.

Various individuals within a school can use the parallels differently. A classroom teacher can use the parallels separately for different purposes, or teachers can work collectively—within grade levels, across grade levels, or across subjects—to use the parallels to support the learning for all, some, or a few students. Furthermore, classroom teachers can use the parallels to modify learning opportunities for students who need something beyond the grade-level curriculum.

What is the driving force behind decisions about when and how to use the parallels? Decisions stem from teacher expertise, the learning goals, and, most important, the students themselves. We draw on the parallels to make curriculum more meaningful, emotive, powerful, engaging, and more likely to energetically advance the abilities and talents of students.

The PCM holds the power to help students and teachers "see the whole" of what they are learning. It is our hope that curriculum based on this model will optimize student learning and enhance the likelihood that all students will lead productive and fulfilling lives. We invite practitioners to read more about this model and join us on a professional journey that we believe will yield that joy and wisdom that comes from seeing the whole. The possibilities are limitless.

THE FORMAT

The curriculum books that are part of our latest initiative share four features that will provide common threads to readers as they transition among the publications. First, each unit contains a section called **Background Information** that provides readers with a snapshot of the lessons or unit. If a series of lessons are provided—instead of a whole unit of study—the author may suggest ways to incorporate the subset of lessons into a larger unit. The author may also identify the parallel(s) she has elected to emphasize and her rationale for highlighting the Core Curriculum and/or the Curriculums of Connections, Practice, or Identity. Authors may share their experiences regarding the best time to teach the unit, such as the beginning of the year or well into the last half of the year. Finally, the author may share what students are expected to know before the unit is taught, as well as resources that would support the teaching and learning activities.

The second common element is the **Content Framework**. One of the "nonnegotiables" of PCM units is that they lead students explicitly to a conceptual understanding of the topics and disciplines on which they are based. Thus, each set of lessons or unit contains a list of concepts, skills, and principles that drive the teaching and learning activities. We also include the national standards addressed in each unit and lesson.

Unit Assessments is the third common feature. Within this section, authors have the opportunity to describe the assessments that are included within their lessons. Some authors, especially those who supplied an entire unit of study, include pre-assessments that align with a performance-based post-assessment. All authors have included formative assessments. Naturally, scoring rubrics are included with these assessments. In many cases, authors describe the nature of students' misconceptions that surface when these performance measures are used, as well as some tips on how to address students' mistaken beliefs.

The final common element is the **two-column format** for organizing the lessons. In the left-hand column, authors sequence the instruction in a step-by-step manner. In the right-hand column, readers will hear the author's voice as he thinks "out loud" about the introduction, teaching and learning activities, and closure. Authors provide many different kinds of information in the right-hand column including, for example, teaching tips, information about student misconceptions, and suggestions on how to differentiate for above-grade-level or below-grade-level students.

OUR INVITATION . . .

We invite you to peruse and implement these curriculum lessons and units. We believe the use of these lessons will be enhanced to the extent that you do the following:

- *Study PCM.* Read the original book, as well as other companion volumes, including *The Parallel Curriculum in the Classroom: Units for Application Across the Content Areas, K–12* and *The Parallel Curriculum in the Classroom: Essays for Application Across the Content Areas, K–12*, and *The Parallel Curriculum Multimedia Kit*. By studying the model in depth, teachers and administrators will have a clear sense of its goals and purposes.

- *Join us on our continuing journey to refine these curriculum units.* We know better than to suggest that these units are scripts for total success in the classroom. They are, at best, our most-thoughtful thinking to date. They are solid evidence that we need to persevere. In small collaborative and reflective teams of practitioners, we invite you to field-test these units and make your own refinements.

- *Raise questions about curriculum materials.* Provocative, compelling, and pioneering questions about the quality of curriculum material—and their incumbent learning opportunities—are essential. Persistent and thoughtful questioning will lead us to the development of strenuous learning opportunities that will contribute to our students' lifelong success in the 21st century.

- *Compare the units with material developed using other curriculum models.* Through such comparisons, we are better able to make decisions about the use of the model and its related curriculum materials for addressing the unique needs of diverse learners.

THE MATH BOOK, GRADES 6–12

This volume contains four units and sets of lessons.

The first unit, **Equivalent Fractions and Partitioning Sets: Keys to Success in Higher-Level Mathematics, Grades 6–7**, is designed for students in Grade 6 or 7. It was designed by Helen Weingart to address the misconceptions and confusion that many middle school students have with relation to fractions. It contains four highly interactive lessons that require a minimum of 10 days; the lessons focus on two major concepts: equivalence and rate of change. These sets of lessons emphasize two parallels: the Core Curriculum and the Curriculum of Practice.

The second unit, **Linear Programming: A Key to Decision Making, Grades 9–10**, by Marianne Cavanaugh, was created for high school freshmen and sophomores. Marianne, a mathematics teacher for more than 25 years, believes that the lessons could also be used for above-grade-level eighth graders. This set of three lessons focuses on linear modeling, a process in which students graph discrete and continuous sets of real-world data. Graphing real-world data provides opportunities for students to discuss and develop deep understanding about domain, range, continuous versus discrete data, and outliers. Throughout the lessons, a large percentage of time is devoted to student discussion about the meaning of the data and how to use data to make informed decisions, thereby becoming the practicing professional. This set of lessons—which illustrates both the Core Curriculum parallel and the Curriculum of Practice—requires a minimum of two weeks to complete.

The third unit in this volume is a geometry unit by Amy Germundson, **Similarity: A Study in Relationships, Grade 10**. Although it is based on the Core Curriculum, the Curriculum of Practice and the Curriculum of Connections also come to the forefront. Throughout the four lessons that require at least two weeks, students are asked to identify and generalize about **relationships**, the unit's organizing macroconcept. As mathematicians, students learn to select tools and the appropriate resources to approach mathematical problems, as well as to state and justify hypotheses. The macroconcepts, **relationships** and **similarity**, also serve as a springboard into the Curriculum of Connections. Students are invited to see how experts in architecture and literature use proportional reasoning as a form of communication in their respective fields.

The final unit focuses on quadratic relationships: **Quadratic Relationships: A Middle School Unit in Algebra, Grade 8**, by Carrie Heaney. It is designed for Grade 8 students. In this unit, students are asked to "think like mathematicians." In the process of discovering what a quadratic relationship exemplifies, students analyze the world outside their classrooms to find quadratic relationships, and then pose questions about these relationships that they will solve using the strategies they are taught in the unit. Throughout the 10 lessons, the goal of this unit is to move students from the mindset of "When am I ever going to use this?" to one where they can start to see the connections between the ideas that they are studying and the value that this mathematical knowledge provides them in solving real-world problems.

SUGGESTED READINGS

Burns, K. (1990). *The Civil War*. Video series. New York: PBS.

Tomlinson, C. A., Kaplan, S. N., Purcell, J., Leppien, J., Burns, D. E., & Strickland, C. A., (2006a). *The parallel curriculum in the classroom, Book 1: Essays for application across the content areas, K–12*. Thousand Oaks, CA: Corwin.

Tomlinson, C. A., Kaplan, S. N., Purcell, J., Leppien, J., Burns, D. E., & Strickland, C. A. (2006b). *The parallel curriculum in the classroom, Book 2: Units for application across the content areas, K–12*. Thousand Oaks, CA: Corwin.

Tomlinson, C. A., Kaplan, S. N., Renzulli, J. S., Purcell, J., Leppien, J., & Burns, D. E. (2002). *The parallel curriculum: A design to develop high potential and challenge high-ability learners*. Thousand Oaks, CA: Corwin.

Tomlinson, C. A., Kaplan, S. N., Renzulli, J. S., Purcell, J., Leppien, J., Burns, D. E., Strickland, C. A., & Imbeau, M. B. (2008). *The parallel curriculum: A design to develop high potential and challenge high-ability learners* (2nd ed.). Thousand Oaks, CA: Corwin.

Tomlinson, C. A., Kaplan, S. N., Renzulli, J. S., Purcell, J., Leppien, J., Burns, D. E., Strickland, C. A., & Imbeau, M. B. (2009). *The parallel curriculum multimedia kit: A design to develop learner potential and challenge advanced learners* (2nd ed.). Thousand Oaks, CA: Corwin.

Young, E. (1992). *Seven blind mice*. http://www2.youseemore.com/anchoragesd/hottitles.asp?loc=2&isbn=0399222618&Author=Ed+Young&Title=Seven+Blind+Mice.

1

Equivalent Fractions and Partitioning Sets

Keys to Success in Higher-Level Mathematics, Grades 6–7

Helen Weingart

INTRODUCTION TO THE UNIT

Proficiency with fractions is an important foundation for learning more-advanced mathematics. My own experience and conversations with teachers of mathematics, including teachers of Advanced Placement calculus and statistics, indicate that fractions are a major source of confusion, error, and misconceptions for our students. This unit uses geometry as a tool to eliminate these areas of confusion and promote an understanding of fractions. Geometry is a unique but accessible way to develop an understanding of a range of fraction concepts; also, it connects with a core component of calculus.

This unit focuses on two major concepts that span several areas in mathematics. These concepts are equivalence and rate of change.

The idea that things can be partitioned or split into parts of equal size underpins the concept of fractions. Being able to partition into any number of parts is the significant link between multiplication, division, and fractions, and fractions are reciprocal with geometric understanding. Students often lose sight of the equivalence concept when partitioning different geometric shapes. They tend to focus on the "size" rather than the "amount" of the region.

Although students often can be taught fairly quickly to produce equivalent fractions by rote, they usually have little understanding of what they are doing or why.

A process based on extensive experience with partitioning quantities by physically or mentally repartitioning materials builds the understanding of what equivalence of fractions means. The goal is to teach students to visualize fractional parts, and later teach them to generalize to a technique for producing equivalent fractions by computation when visualizing is difficult.

The second area of focus in this unit is the concept of rate of change. This is a novel way to look at fractions; it leads directly to a fundamental understanding of linear functions in algebra. Students need to extend their understanding of fractions insofar as it can represent rate of change. Students can algorithmically state that 1 of 4 cookies is equivalent to 2 of 8 cookies and 4 of 16 cookies, and so on, using a "double the numerator, double the denominator" rule. However, should you ask them to complete an equivalence using 4 of 16 with 3 of x, they are perplexed. In explaining to students that the original fraction could be represented on the coordinate plane (up 1 over 4), they find that they can generate a myriad of equivalent rates while projecting denominators if they go up $\frac{1}{2}$ then over 2. This connection to algebra opens the door to deeper understanding as students move along in their mathematical careers.

A key instructional strategy is allowing students to develop their own algorithms. By the time we see students in middle school, they have had experiences with fractions; they may have had little opportunity to develop their own personal algorithms, however, or to extend those strategies to routine fraction procedures. My experience reflects what the research tells us: "[W]hen children are allowed to create and invent, their fertile minds enable them to solve problems in a variety of original and logical ways. When their minds have not been shackled by rules and conventions, children are free to invent procedures that reflect their natural thought processes. . . . [C]hildren can develop sophisticated and meaningful procedures in computation and problem solving without explicit instruction in the use of conventional algorithms" (Kamii and Madell, as quoted in Warrington, 1997).

Finally, a significant underpinning for success with the fraction notations in higher-level mathematics is that students understand that the fraction notation is a shorthand way to show the division sign. It is not unusual for students to struggle to work out the "answer" to 3 ÷ 5, such as when sharing three chocolate bars among five friends, not seeing immediately that each must get $\frac{3}{5}$ of a bar. Geometry is a unique and effective tool that assists students in developing the number sense required to use fractions flexibly.

Students are engaged in activities that provide them with extensive experience in splitting a diverse range of discrete and continuous wholes into equal-sized parts so that they are able to construct a suitable partition even if they are not given a predrawn diagram. The goal is to provide students varied experiences with reasoning about fractions via divided quantities, numerical components, reference points, numerical conversions, and geometric representations, thus enabling students to work successfully with all these interpretations.

A final note: when moving through this unit on fractions, it is extremely important to have the manipulatives for students in place. When students are working independently, they should have manipulatives on their desks. When students are working in groups, the group should have manipulatives within reach. It is common to have manipulatives centrally located in the classroom for student use. While this certainly provides for student learning, it does inhibit students. Think of how a student would feel if he had to go over to the "manipulative center" to get the tiles or counters to complete the activity. Everyone would watch that student go and get the tiles—how embarrassing. In all likelihood, he would not get them at all. By placing manipulatives within the reach of the students, they will reach for them. In reaching for them, they will use them. In using them, they will strengthen their understanding and enhance their Advanced Placement potential.

CONTENT FRAMEWORK

Discipline-Specific Concepts

C1: Equivalence

C2: Rate of change

C3: Part-part-whole relationships

C4: Partitioning

C5: Equivalent rates of change

C6: Ratio

C7: Set interpretation

C8: Region models

C9: Complex fractions

Principles and Generalizations

P1: Fractions describe parts of a whole. The whole can be an object, a collection, or a quantity. Fractions represent parts of discrete quantities (collections of objects).

P2: The size of a fractional part is based on the size of the unit. Equal parts need not look alike, but they must have the same size or amount of the relevant quantity.

P3: The fraction notation is used to represent a rate, a ratio, and a proportional relationship.

P4: A fraction notation can represent either an additive $\left(\frac{3}{4} = \frac{1}{4} + \frac{1}{4} + \frac{1}{4}\right)$ or multiplicative relationship: $\frac{3}{4} = 3\left(\frac{1}{4}\right)$.

P5: Models help students clarify ideas that are often confused when explored in a purely symbolic form.

P6: The same fractional quantity can be represented by many different fractions.

P7: Even though set size varies, when fractions are equivalent, the rate of change is constant.

P8: Equivalent fractions are two ways of describing the same amount by using different-sized fractional parts.

P9: A fraction also represents a rate of change.

P10: Rate of change describes the relationship between two variables. It tells us the slope of the line. Slope is a very important ratio in algebra.

P11: Rate of change is used to analyze real-world phenomena, make predictions, and assess possible outcomes.

P12: A variety of models can be used to represent wholes and parts of wholes.

P13: Fraction names represent the relationship between parts and wholes.

P14: Drawings (models) do not speak for themselves. The same diagram of a divided quantity can represent many different relationships, depending on how the whole is defined. (Different amounts can represent a whole. Different wholes make different fractional parts in the same model.)

P15: Making equivalent rates of change is the foundation for the algorithm for complex fractions.

P16: A ratio is a number that relates two quantities or measures in a given situation in a multiplicative relationship (in contrast to a difference or additive relationship).

P17: Ratios compare any two amounts that can be parts of the same whole, wholes, or parts of different wholes.

P18: A fraction symbol can be used to represent a division or ratio relationship between quantities.

P19: There is a link between fractions and division. A fraction is another way of expressing division: $2 \div 3$, $\frac{2}{3}$, and $\frac{1}{3}$ of 2 all mean the same thing.

Skills

S1: Develop an intuitive sense of the magnitude of fractional numbers.

S2: Choose and describe the most efficient strategy to solve problems with commonly used fractions.

S3: Use mental math to solve simple problems with commonly used fractions.

S4: Create and describe mathematical rules (algorithms) for a wide variety of patterns.

S5: Recognize that a fraction describes the pattern that is a rate of change.

S6: Interpret rate of change from graphical and numerical data.

S7: Learn how to graphically represent rate of change.

S8: Locate, identify, and order fractions on the coordinate plane.

S9: Understand the "meaning" of numerator and denominator.

S10: Use physical objects and visual models to represent a whole when given a fractional part, or to represent a fractional part when given the whole.

S11: Develop and verbalize mathematical rules that describe patterns that represent equivalent amounts in sets of different sizes.

S12: Simplify fractions to represent rates of change.

S13: Recognize that a fraction bar is a grouping symbol: $\dfrac{2+3}{3+4} = (2+3) \div (3+4)$.

S14: Build models and draw diagrams to describe the relationship between fractions.

S15: Describe the difference between fractions and ratios.

S16: Decompose fractions into factors.

S17: Write numerical representations for geometric representations of fraction sets.

S18: Interpret a fraction that has a fraction in the numerator or denominator or both.

Standards

The concepts, principles, and skills included with this unit reflect the national standards adopted by the National Council of Teachers of Mathematics (NCTM). These standards are listed below:

1. Compute fluently and make reasonable estimates.

2. Select appropriate methods and tools for computing with fractions and decimals from among mental computation, estimation, calculators or computers, and paper and pencil, depending on the situation; apply the elected methods.

3. Develop and analyze algorithms for computing with fractions, decimals, and integers, and develop fluency in their use.

4. Develop and use strategies to estimate the results of rational-number computations and judge the reasonableness of results.

5. Apply and adapt a variety of appropriate strategies to solve problems.

6. Communicate mathematical thinking coherently and clearly to peers, teachers, and others.

7. Analyze and evaluate the mathematical thinking and strategies of others.

8. Use the language of mathematics to express precisely mathematical ideas.

9. Analyze functions of one variable by investigating rates of change, intercepts, zeros, asymptotes, and local and global behavior.

10. Investigate how a change in one variable relates to a change in a second variable.

11. Identify and describe situations with constant or varying rates of change and compare them.

12. Create and describe mental images of objects, patterns, and paths.

13. Use geometric models to represent and explain numerical and algebraic relationships.

14. Use geometric models to gain insights into and answer questions in other areas of mathematics.

15. Use graphs to analyze the nature of changes in quantities in linear relationships. Approximate and interpret rates of change from graphical and numerical data.

This Unit and the Parallel Curriculum Model

Within the context of the Parallel Curriculum Model, these lessons on fractions focus primarily on the Core Parallel and the Curriculum of Practice. The concepts and principles about fractions presented here are basic to the discipline, thereby aligning it to the Core Curriculum. The lessons help students answer general questions such as, What does this information mean? Why does this information matter? Do these ideas make sense in my life? Furthermore, the lessons are organized in a way that facilitates students' ability to remember, make meaning, and use what they know as they journey toward expertise in mathematics.

These lessons also reflect the Curriculum of Practice because the learning activities invite students to engage in the work of practicing professionals. Mathematicians deal with problems, determine meaningful patterns of information within the problem, seek strategies for solving the problem, and communicate their findings. Students who complete these lessons will find themselves asking questions such as, What tools and skills does the mathematician use? How does a practitioner approach problems like these? On what basis does a mathematician draw conclusions? Other, more-specific questions for these lessons on fractions are listed below.

Core Curriculum

1. What are we communicating when we use a fraction? What does it mean to have equal shares of something?

2. How can we tell if we have equal shares if the sizes of the pieces are different?

3. Why do we use mathematical rules? What do those rules tell us?

4. Is there more than one rule that could be used to describe a pattern?

5. How much is "one"?

6. What does it mean to use the fraction bar as a grouping symbol?

7. How can we (or, What does it mean to) decompose numbers using either multiplication or addition?

8. How does rate of change help us understand the world around us?

9. How does a ratio compare to fractions?

10. Is decomposing fractions the same as decomposing whole numbers?

11. How do the patterns generated by complex fractions compare to the patterns generated by simple fractions?

Curriculum of Practice

1. What is a mathematical model?

2. Why are models important in mathematics?

3. How are models used in the "real world"?

4. How can we use mental math to make complex fractions easy to understand?

5. How does rate of change help us understand the world around us?

6. Why is it important to be able to partition flexibly?

ASSESSMENTS

This series of mathematics lessons contains a matched pre- and post-assessment. Furthermore, the items on the matched pre- and post-assessment have been purposefully created to assess important concepts and understandings. The first 21 items on the pre-assessment and post-assessment measure a student's flexibility to interpret fractions. Items 1, 2, and 6, for example, illustrate traditional ways to represent fractions. Items 3, 5, and 19–21, on the other hand, are nontraditional ways, and incorporate common and complex fractional notation. These latter examples will require students to "stretch" their thinking about the meaning of fractions. Items 22–30 are designed to assess a student's understanding of equivalency. Items 34–39 elicit a student's understanding and flexibility in representing fractions within the context of geometry. Finally, Items 40–42 assess a student's emerging sense of factors and multiples.

The data collected from the pre- and post-assessment will provide teachers with evidence of overall student growth, as well as students' deepening understanding related to specific concepts. By measuring student pre- and post-data on a cluster of items such as equivalency, for example (Items 22–30), a teacher might decide that he will reteach that part of the unit or change the instructional approach next time he works through this set of lessons. Disaggregating the data by cluster provides teachers with powerful data to either maintain instructional practices or differentiate their instructional repertoire based on students' learning needs.

Besides the pre- and post-assessment, there are countless other opportunities embedded within these lessons for teachers to "check the weather" in their classrooms. Class worksheets, student discussions, and homework assignments are all critical sources of information about students' understandings and misconceptions. As such, each is an important source of formative assessment data that practitioners can use to customize instruction to the whole class, small groups of students, or individuals.

It is important for readers to note that many suggestions for differentiation are incorporated into these lessons. These suggestions are based on many years of experience with middle school mathematics students. These "general" reflections on above-grade-level learners, on-grade-level learners, and below-grade-level learners can be coupled with the reader's knowledge of her students as they progress through these lessons, as well as the specific information that each student has gleaned from the formative assessments contained herein.

UNIT SEQUENCE, DESCRIPTION, AND TEACHER REFLECTIONS

The idea that things can be partitioned or split into parts of equal size underpins the fraction concept. The ability to partition any number is the significant link among multiplication, division, and fractions, and is reciprocal with geometric understanding. Students need extensive experience in splitting a diverse range of discrete and continuous wholes into equal-sized parts. They need experiences that help them understand that the whole they are describing a part of can be an object, a collection, or a quantity.

Another key understanding students need to develop is that the same fractional quantity can be represented with many different fractions. Although students can often be taught fairly quickly to produce equivalent fractions by rote, they usually have little understanding of what they are doing or why. A process based on extensive experience with partitioning quantities by physically or mentally repartitioning materials builds the understanding of what equivalence of fractions means. The goal is to teach students to visualize fractional parts, and later teach them to generalize to a technique for producing equivalent fractions by computation when visualizing is difficult.

Finally, a significant underpinning for success with the fraction notations in higher-level mathematics is student understanding that the fraction notation is a shorthand way to show the division sign. Research tells us that this important relationship between fractions and division is often overlooked by both students and adults. Many will struggle to work out the "answer" to $3 \div 5$, such as when sharing three chocolate bars among five friends, not seeing immediately that each must get $\frac{3}{5}$ of a bar. The approach in this volume is designed to assist students to develop the number sense required to use fractions flexibly.

LESSON 1.1: EXPLORING EQUIVALENT FRACTIONS

Length: Two days

Unit Sequence	Teacher Reflections
Concepts C1, C2	There are two areas of focus to consider in this unit: equivalence and rate of change. Students are able to partition different geometric shapes but lose sight of the equivalence concept. For example, they partition a rectangle into fourths, and then similarly partition a circle into fourths. There is confusion about $\frac{1}{4}$ of a rectangle and $\frac{1}{4}$ of a circle. Students are focused on only the "size" of the region rather than the partition that $\frac{1}{4}$ of that region represents. Although it is true that $\frac{1}{4}$ of a pound is a different quantity from $\frac{1}{4}$ of a ton, the understanding of $\frac{1}{4}$ is what is germane to student conceptual development. The implications of equivalence extend beyond common-sized partitions. Middle school students often struggle when they are presented with a shape that has eight equal-sized partitions and a shape with four equal-sized partitions. Students are often perplexed if the first region has three of the eight partitions shaded and the student is asked to shade in an equivalent amount in the region with 4 partitions. Students do not "partition" the first region as $\frac{2}{8} + \frac{1}{8}$, extending their understanding to $\frac{1}{4} + \frac{1}{2}$ of $\frac{1}{4}$. Truly, this understanding is the linch pin for advanced mathematical understanding. The second area of focus in this unit is a fraction as a representation of a rate of change. This is a novel way to look at fractions, one that leads directly to a fundamental understanding of linear functions in algebra. Students need to extend their understanding of fractions in that they represent numerous interpretations (constructs), representations (models), and coding conventions $\left(\frac{5}{4}, 1\frac{1}{4}, 1.25, 125\% \right)$ and can represent a rate of change. Students can algorithmically state that 1 of 4 cookies is equivalent to 2 of 8 cookies and 4 of 16 cookies, and so on, using a "double the numerator, double the denominator" rule. However, if you ask them to complete an equivalence using a relationship such as 4 of 16 as it relates to the relationship 3 to x, they are perplexed.

Unit Sequence	Teacher Reflections
	In explaining to students that the original fraction could be represented on the coordinate plane as a variety of rates—"up 4 over 16" or perhaps "up 2 over 8," and so on—they find that they can generate a myriad of equivalent rates while projecting denominators. The accelerated learner can be challenged with the complex relationship of "up $\frac{1}{2}$ over 2," and can compare that rate of change to the original 4 of 16. These concepts, equivalence, and rate of change provide the connection to algebra and will open the door to deeper understanding as students move along in their mathematical careers.
Principles P1, P2, P6, P7, P8, P9, P10, P11	As we develop the concepts of equivalence and rate of change in students, it is important to realize that students are not necessarily "organized" in the traditional ways that teachers have come to expect. This is developed extensively in the narrative section, Day 1 and Day 2. This organizational issue is an important component in developing a conceptual understanding of fractions that goes beyond an algorithmic understanding; this understanding can best be mastered with manipulatives, working on graph paper, or both. When working with graph paper, you can give the dimensions for the region and ensure that students have the "exact"-sized region. While we can draw a square on the board that may look, in fact, somewhat rectangular, as adults, we can flexibly recharacterize that shape to be "square." Take the time to think of a student who is tentative and is not able to flexibly recharacterize that shape as a square. In fact, that student may be so distracted by the lack of precision that the lesson is lost to him. The manipulatives or graph paper, or both, can circumvent that distraction. Choose appropriate region dimensions for beginning activities so that the geometric partitions can be easily shaded and reconfigured. Activities such as these provide an opportunity for the teacher to engage in quality formative assessment of students. The ease or difficulty with which students adapt to the visual reconfiguration may redirect your focus. If students are struggling, additional time may be warranted, or a more formal process of partitioning included. Make sure that students can master the visual. Deep understanding of the reconfigurations extends to concepts involving geometric probability in the "fair, not fair" games.
Skills S1, S2, S3, S4	
Standards SD3, SD4, SD5, SD6, SD7, SD8, SD9, SD10, SD11, SD12, SD13, SD14	

Unit Sequence	Teacher Reflections
Guiding Questions 1. What does it mean to have equal shares of something? 2. How can we tell if we have equal shares if the sizes of the pieces are different? 3. How does rate of change help us understand the world around us? 4. Why do we use mathematical rules? What do they tell us? 5. Is there more than one rule that could be used to describe a pattern? 6. What are we communicating when we use a fraction?	It is extremely important to have the manipulatives for students in place. When students are working independently, they should have manipulatives on their desks. When they are working in groups, the group should have manipulatives within reach. While having manipulatives centrally located in the classroom for student use may provide for convenience of classroom management, it also may inhibit students. Self-conscious middle school students will not go over to the "manipulative center" to get the tiles or counters they need to complete activities. If teachers place manipulatives close to the students, they reach for them. In reaching for them, they use them, and they strengthen and enhance their understanding of the underlying concepts.

Introduction
 	
Use **Resource 1.1: Pre-Assessment: What Did You Learn About Fractions?**
 	
   These lessons develop core knowledge and awareness of fraction patterns necessary for application in an algebraic context. This understanding is the precursor to "partitioning," which is the significant link between multiplication, division, and fractions, and is reciprocal with geometric understanding. These two lessons are designed to explore equivalent fractions in sets of different sizes and to introduce students to the idea that a fraction represents both quantity and rate of change.
   Students will identify fractional parts of sets and plot the unreduced fractions in given sets to form lines.
	Two to three weeks ahead of time, ask students to complete the pre-assessment that is included at the end of this lesson. Remind students that they are *not* expected to know the answers to these questions. Instead, you will use the data from their work to tailor your instruction to their learning needs. The pre-assessment should take approximately 30 minutes. Refer to the Introduction section to this unit for additional information about the pre-assessment and post-assessment.
	   It is key for students to have opportunities to explore partitioning of sets into whole sets and fractional sets; this partitioning is the concept behind writing an improper fraction as a mixed number. There are two issues that come up continually in algebra and advanced mathematics: the use of the fraction bar and reducing fractions to their lowest terms. When presented with the problem of simplifying the expression $\frac{6x + 2}{2}$, students incorrectly give the answer $3x + 2$ or $3x$, even going so far as to say $\frac{6 + 2}{2} = 5 \text{ or } 7.$
	   Students have difficulty with the notion that the fraction bar is a grouping symbol that means the same as the parentheses in the distributive property, and with the idea that dividing by a number or an expression is equivalent to multiplying by its reciprocal. For example, $\frac{8}{4} = \frac{1}{4} \times 8$, or, in algebra, $\frac{2x - 6}{2} = \frac{1}{2}(2x - 6)$ are examples of using the fraction bar as a grouping symbol. The activities throughout the unit support the development of this understanding.
	   Another significant misconception that we often see in algebra is the expression $\frac{x + 3}{x + 4}$ incorrectly simplified to $\frac{3}{4}$.

Unit Sequence	Teacher Reflections
	This misconception relates directly to how fractions are reduced to the simplest terms by factoring out the greatest common factor. Because students do not really understand the algorithm, they are unable to apply it to algebraic expressions.
Teaching Strategies and Learning Experiences *Day 1* Use **Resource 1.2: Recognizing Equivalent Fractions: What Fraction of Each Set Is Shaded?** as a warm-up for the group activities. Plot each set on a single grid, then plot A and B on a second grid using a different color for Set A and Set B. (Use **Resource 1.3: Overhead Template.**) Students should realize that these are all the same fraction in different forms. *Teacher Note.* When the fractions are plotted in unreduced form, they will form a line with a rate of change of $\frac{1}{4}$. Use this concept when facilitating the discussion that follows. *Day 2* The second part of this lesson is a similar exploration of different equivalent fractions. It is designed for use as a small-group activity. Use **Resource 1.2: Recognizing Equivalent Fractions: What Fraction of Each Set Is Shaded?** If students plot the graphs on overhead transparencies (see **Resource 1.3: Overhead Template**), comparisons can easily be made among the different fractions. Depending on the levels within groups, students can continue exploring the rate of change notion with a variety of options; for example, (1) fractions can be selected that are common fractions; (2) complex fractions can be selected and introduced; and (3) fractions can be selected that explore the use of negative values in the numerator or denominator, as appropriate.	On the surface, this may seem to be a very simple activity. However, it is often the simple concepts that we take for granted. The algorithm is so easy to present. The first concept is simply representing equivalent fraction pieces in each box. If you look at the worksheet, you will see that the circles are not shaded using a traditional shading pattern. This is intentional. The shading method of the circles does not seem as neat and organized as one would like. In doing this activity, use overhead chips in two colors and ask students if they like the way the dark chips are organized. You can discuss the pros and cons of the arrangement of the dark chips. Now is a good time to ask if there are other ways to arrange the dark and light chips to make the task easier. Is it important for every child to model $\frac{1}{4}$ similarly? No—but it is important to realize that there is *no* correct way, as long as the students understand that $\frac{1}{4}$ is dark in each case. Spending time discussing this visual equivalency model will develop refined visual skills in students (see Item 2 under in the Content Framework that is in the Introduction to this unit). Spending time on this will ensure success for the right-hand side of the page, because some students may use a nontraditional coloring pattern. In addressing the issue of fractional representations in the lesson, there will be more freedom for the learner to create his representation for the fraction. This flexibility allows the teacher to enhance student understanding while authenticating a child's way of knowing and learning. The algorithm is far less flexible than modeling. As you continue with **Resource 1.2: Recognizing Equivalent Fractions: What Fraction of Each Set Is Shaded?**, the graphing component will come into play. You will now be graphing the fractions. You can see that only the first quadrant is provided. At this point, we are talking about fractions and their relationship to rates of change. (Depending on the level of your students, you can have a discussion about moving into Quadrant III, including the concept of domain; this is a perfect opportunity to differentiate for the accelerated learner.) In workshops with teachers, the graphing of a fraction appears to be counterintuitive to their understanding.

Unit Sequence	Teacher Reflections
A separate student worksheet is included to use for individual work. See **Resource 1.4: What Fraction Is Shaded?**	The focus of the plotting of points is designed to develop slope. The *y*-axis is deliberately set as the numerator value and the *x*-axis is set as the denominator. The grids are labeled accordingly, so as to avoid any errors in plotting the fraction. After students create their graphs, use the following questions to guide the students to the understanding that a fraction is also a rate of change. 1. Looking at the points in Set A, how can we get from one point to the next? Is there a pattern? 2. Is that pattern the same for Set B? How are they the same? How are they different? Indicate to the students that change is moving up or down, and that the change is constant. Change represents what is shaded. A fraction is *also* a rate of change. This is different from representing an equal share of something. Understanding that a fraction is also a rate of change will help students be successful in higher-level mathematics. There is also the opportunity to discuss "up and over to the right" relating that to "down then left." This can be a rich discussion for the class: integers and fractions as division. **Resource 1.4: What Fraction Is Shaded?** can be group work or individual work as is appropriate for the class or individual students. The first two pages are simply a review. The third page is the crucial piece, and time should be spent going over those answers. There may be some difficulty in developing an algebraic rule. Use an intuitive approach; that approach is the emphasis for the entire unit. Depending on the group, you can begin discussions such as $\frac{1}{3} \cdot x$, where *x* represents one $\left(\frac{1}{1}, \frac{2}{2}, \frac{3}{3}\right)$. Since this is no longer the algorithm for multiplication, it now represents what is happening on the grid, so students can internalize the notion of equivalency, and thus develop understanding. This is also a connection for the multiplication algorithm. It is also appropriate to incorporate vocabulary such as the multiplicative identity element. Students can relate fractional equivalency to the fact that they started with one fraction, then generated a second fraction by using a rate of change, then a third, and so on. Students now have an opportunity to discover fractional equivalency using a nonlinguistic representation that uses a rate of change model (i.e., slope). Depending on the group, you may wish to talk about representing one as $\frac{1}{2}$ over $\frac{1}{2}$ to see what they will propose as a solution. Their answers can be "checked" using the grid. This is a very concrete way to develop the

Unit Sequence	Teacher Reflections
	notion of complex fractions that routinely occur in upper-level mathematics. **Resource 1.5: Fractions and Rates of Change** is designed to be a homework sheet, reinforcing the skills, concepts, and discussions that are developed during the lessons.
Closure Students work in small groups to summarize their responses to questions on **Resource 1.4: What Fraction Is Shaded?** Groups will be assigned to report their results for fraction sets A, B, and C. Review with students the connection between the rate of change and a fraction: • What fraction of each set is shaded? • What fraction of the set is not shaded? • What is the rule you used for determining the shaded part? • What is the rule you used for determining the unshaded part? • If you combine the shaded and unshaded parts, what is the result? • What is the rate of change?	

LESSON 1.2: EXPLORING FRACTIONAL PARTITIONS

Length: Two days

Unit Sequence	Teacher Reflections
Concepts C3, C4, C5	
Principles P1, P3, P4, P5, P6, P12, P13, P14, P15	As fraction understanding emerges, we move to a real-world understanding of fractions and partitioning. Repeated opportunities for modeling the partitioning will provide the scaffold for learning that heretofore has been overlooked in middle school. It is very easy for the teacher to move to the algorithm, and arguably even easier to just show it. I have been surprised to see that students who know the algorithm can still struggle to model the mathematics of that algorithm. In all cases, be sure that the students model all the situations. The second part of this lesson requires a deep understanding of fractions; modeling in this second part is key.
Skills S5, S6, S7, S8	
Standards SD1, SD3, SD4, SD5, SD8, SD10, SD11, SD15	
Guiding Questions 1. How does what we know about basic number relationships (e.g., the same number can be represented in many different ways: $6 + 3 = 9$, $5 + 4 = 9$, and so on) help us understand fractions? 2. Why do we need to be able to break a group into different-sized pieces? 3. How much is "one"? 4. What does it mean to use the fraction bar as a grouping symbol?	

Unit Sequence	Teacher Reflections
Background Overview *Exploring Fractional Partitions Using Lemon Cookies* Students are introduced to partitioning using fractions (sets) that are familiar to them. They translate the visual representation into complex fractions and move on to investigate the rate of change for the complex fractions. *Teacher Note.* Making equivalent rates of change is the foundation for the algorithm for complex fractions.	Surprisingly, teachers I have worked with find this to be a challenging activity. Their tendency is to immediately use the algorithm without modeling. When they are directed to use modeling, they are tentative when they get to Question 3 of **Resource 1.6: Lemon Cookies**. Teachers need time to discover that they can "cut the cookies in half." Once this is discovered, the discussion needs to focus on the part-whole component essential to fraction understanding. Additionally, the teachers are further consternated with Example 4. Again, further development of the part-whole relationship is the emphasis for the lesson.
Introduction Students explore partitioning sets by starting with a hands-on exploration in a familiar context: eating cookies. The focus of this activity is on the problem-solving process, not on the algorithm. **Resource 1.6: Lemon Cookies** should be used as a whole-class exploration. **Resource 1.7: Our Favorites: Chocolate and Vanilla Cookies** can be used as a group assignment (for all students) or as an individual assignment.	Refrain from using this activity as a worksheet for multiplication. Using the worksheet in that fashion results in a 10-minute task for students that simply requires the application of the algorithm for multiplication. Modeling is the key here. Students at both ends of the spectrum need a modeling experience. Students at the lower level comfortably complete these problems, with some students at the upper end struggling to create a model. My experience is that some students who know the algorithm cannot model the situation—after all, these are the very same problems that had teachers stumped. This is an indicator that those students have not internalized a true understanding of fractions.
Teaching Strategies and Learning Experiences *Day 1* It is important that each student have 18 paper circles and scissors **(Resource 1.8: Cookies Template)**. To guide students through the activity, start with the thirds.	This activity, **Resource 1.6: Lemon Cookies**, is designed to provide an option for novel problem solving with fractions. For this activity, the students have a single group—lemon cookies—with which to work. It is crucial that students have disks or use the cookie cutouts for this activity **(Resource 1.8: Cookies Template)**. It is the manipulation of the "cookies" that will develop the deep understanding that students need to progress in mathematics. The teacher needs to have "overhead" disks to model answers and solving strategies for the students. I would suggest that you bring in envelopes so that the "cookies" can go into the envelopes for later use.

Unit Sequence	Teacher Reflections
Day 2 **Resource 1.7: Our Favorites: Chocolate and Vanilla Cookies** can be done as a class. It is important that students see that each box represents one-third of a whole even though the picture may lead students to think they are dividing the bars into eighths, fifths, and thirds, respectively. Make sure the students have 12 disks representing vanilla and 24 disks representing chocolate **(Resource 1.8: Cookies Template)**. Be sure *all* students have the circle models and scissors to aid in their understanding.	During instruction, use the terminology "groups of" rather than "packs," because the idea of packs distracts from building the understanding that we would like the students to acquire. As you move through the unit, you can develop an "algorithm" so that you can express the two-thirds as $\dfrac{2 \text{ groups of } 6}{3 \text{ groups of } 6}$ so that students can see $\dfrac{2 \cdot 6}{3 \cdot 6}$ as $\dfrac{2}{3}$. You can continue this modeling through the other examples. As indicated earlier, it is crucial for advanced mathematical thinking that students understand the difference between $\dfrac{6 + 6}{6 + 6 + 6} \neq \dfrac{0}{6}$, which is a typical error when students see the rational expression versions of this fraction concept. This development can occur during the Lemon Cookie activity. As you continue with the lesson, students may view **Resource 1.7: Our Favorites: Chocolate and Vanilla Cookies** as being more challenging. The students must use the cookie cutouts **(Resource 1.8: Cookies Template)** to model the situations to arrive at the answers. Students can be quite creative in their representations. Allow students to model their solutions on the overhead using overhead disks in two colors. There are times when this "sharing" of solutions is short-circuited. It is important to take the time so that all the solutions are modeled, particularly if students have represented the solutions differently. This provides the opportunities for the visual and kinesthetic learner to achieve understanding.
Closure Students complete **Resource 1.9: Tiling the Family Room** for homework. Again, have students summarize for the class. The student-created problems will synthesize their understanding. Ask the students to create examples that are different from the cookie and tiles examples.	**Resource 1.9: Tiling the Family Room** is designed as a homework sheet for the students. The challenge question is to have the students design their own examples. This is a time to talk about factors, multiples, prime numbers, abundant numbers (factors of the number add to a value greater than the number), and deficient numbers (factors of the number add to a value less than the number) as appropriate with your students. This vocabulary should be integrated into the explanations the next day. Students will be developing algorithms without any "real" lesson for algorithms. They just will apply logical reasoning, and will then own the algorithm.

LESSON 1.3: FRACTURED FRACTIONS

Length: Two days

Unit Sequence	Teacher Reflections

Day 1: **Resource 1.10: Modeling Fractions,** and **Resource 1.11: Working With Fractions**
 	
Day 2: **Resource 1.12: Fractured Fractions and Beyond**
	Teachers elicited surprise at the focus on complex fractions. I have been asked, "When will students use this?" I found this to be a very interesting comment.
	    Complex fractions occur every day—"I traveled for half an hour at 60 miles per hour" is the easiest example to use. There is also "I lost $\frac{1}{2}$ a pound." Teachers routinely implement dimensional analysis without realizing that they have just converted their "complex" fraction into a proper fraction.
	    In upper-level mathematics, complex fractions are the norm rather than the exception. Those fractions take on the look of one algebraic expression over another, routinely used in developing the derivative and the use of partial fractions during the early units in calculus.

Concepts C6, C7, C8	
Principles P1, P2, P11, P13, P14, P16, P17	
Skills S9, S10, S11, S12, S13	
Standards SD1, SD2, SD3, SD4, SD5, SD14	
Guiding Questions 1. How does a ratio compare to the fractions we studied in our last lesson? 2. How can we decompose numbers using either multiplication or addition? 3. What is a mathematical model? 4. Why are models important in mathematics? 5. How do models help us understand fractional relationships? 6. Is decomposing fractions the same as decomposing whole numbers?	

Unit Sequence	Teacher Reflections

Background Information	The concepts presented in this lesson are significant in the development of algebraic skills. The misconceptions regarding fractions are particularly evident. Students will routinely "cancel" numbers without regard to the fact that they can "cancel" terms only when those terms are factors.
	
	    A fraction cannot be reduced by an addend in the numerator and denominator. It is not typical for students to have experiences with fractions that seem similar such as
	
	$\dfrac{2 \times 6}{2 \times 5}$ versus $\dfrac{2 + (3 + 3)}{2 + (3 + 2)}$. In an algebra class, students will
	
	routinely cancel the addend 2, due in part to a lack of understanding for the reducing algorithm.
	
	    Here is an opportunity to develop understanding. Students who have worked through these problems enjoy providing lots of alternatives that would model the same "answer." A solid understanding of this concept is crucial for students.

Introduction
 	
Students have numerous misconceptions about how fractions can be combined or separated.
    Often in algebra and calculus, students are required to **decompose** fractions into factors in ways with which they are unfamiliar. For example, they understand that
 	
$\dfrac{6}{x} = \dfrac{2 \times 3}{x}$, but they have more
 	
trouble recognizing that $\dfrac{6}{x} = 6\left(\dfrac{1}{x}\right)$.
 	
Make sure students model the steps from the geometric to the numerical representations to eliminate fraction misconceptions.
    A nice extension activity would be to have students categorize the various fraction forms from **Resource 1.10: Modeling Fractions,** Question 2 (Items A–L). This activity can be diagnostic for the teacher if students simply group by operations versus value.
    Students should be able to create four groups: $\left(\dfrac{5}{3}, \dfrac{8}{5}, \dfrac{8}{7}, \dfrac{6}{5}\right)$.
 	
    On Day 2, **Resource 1.12: Fractured Fractions and Beyond** moves from the concrete or visual understanding to the algebraic or algorithmic processes needed for Advanced Placement thinking.
    Resource 1.13: Decomposing Fractions is provided as a homework sheet.
	Resource 1.10: Modeling Fractions seems to be quite obvious to the teacher—so obvious, in fact, that little or no time is devoted to this visual understanding of improper fractions. Students consistently make errors in this simplification process beginning in Algebra 1 continuing through to Calculus. In upper-level math, students look at expressions such as $\dfrac{x^2}{x^2 - 4}$ and "simplify" that expression to either $\dfrac{1}{4}$ or -4. I have even seen this error in calculus students: when they are working with a problem such as $\lim\limits_{x \to 2} \dfrac{x^2}{x^2 - 4}$ they give similar answers: $\dfrac{-1}{4}$ or -4.
	    Hence the inclusion of these worksheets. In all cases, students should model these situations. You can use the cookie cutouts from the previous lessons and model the situations with overhead counters.
	    Resource 1.11: Working With Fractions moves to the conventional fraction form. It is important that students develop the algorithm: *do not* provide the algorithm for them.
	    The worksheet, **Resource 1.12: Fractured Fractions and Beyond**, extends student understanding toward the development of algebraic representation. I would not overemphasize the variables. You will be surprised that the students will just use the variables, perhaps because there are choices available.
	    The triangle area problem is a perfect example to use at this point. When fraction understanding is only algorithmic, students cannot "reconfigure" the algorithm to a nonconforming application. How many times have students looked at $\dfrac{1}{2} \cdot 11 \cdot 10$ going through in order, rather than dividing the 10 by 2 then multiplying by the 11? One could argue that students are troubled with this example, as well—$4 \times 15 \times 25$—and do not notice the 4×25 as the first choice for computing. If, in fact, your students miss this association component, take the time to develop this type of number sense with them.

Unit Sequence	Teacher Reflections
Teaching Strategies and Learning Experiences *Day 1* Using **Resource 1.10: Modeling Fractions,** make sure students model the steps from the geometric to the numerical representations to eliminate fraction misconceptions regarding simplification of fractions.	Modeling fractions as a sum in the numerator or denominator (or both) is one of those activities that can seem so basic that we tend to skim right over it. It cannot be overstated, though, that you do not have to go far to find an algebra teacher who will lament student misunderstandings. Not a day goes by without the following error: $\frac{x+2}{2+1} = \frac{x}{1} = x$. Yet every time this error occurs, the algebra teacher will ask if this is true: $\frac{7}{3} = \frac{5+2}{2+1}$? The students all agree, with an exuberant "Yes!" Then the teacher continues, and asks if this is true: $\frac{5+2}{2+1}$? $=$? $\frac{5}{1}$,? $=$? 5. The students all reply, "No!" Day in and day out, teachers need to repeat this type of example. The need to own this concept cannot be underestimated.
Resource 1.11: Working With Fractions is an appropriate homework assignment. It will reinforce the concepts developed in class. *Day 2* **Resource 1.12: Fractured Fractions and Beyond** moves from the concrete or visual understanding to the algebraic or algorithmic processes needed for Advanced Placement thinking. Students will now look at fraction forms that seem quite similar: $\left(\frac{2+(3\times 2)}{2+(3\times 1)}\right)$ versus $\frac{2+(3+3)}{2+(3+2)}$. It is important to develop concrete understanding of these two concepts. Other skills that are incorporated include an extension to an algebraic understanding in differentiating: $\frac{6}{x} = 6\left(\frac{1}{x}\right)$ versus $\frac{x}{6} = \left(\frac{1}{6}\right)x$. A nice extension activity would be to have students categorize the various fraction forms from **Resource 1.11: Working With Fractions,** Question 2 (Items A–L). You can use this activity as a diagnostic if your students simply group by operations versus value.	**Resource 1.11: Working With Fractions** moves to the conventional fraction form. It is important that students develop the algorithm: *do not* provide the algorithm for them. The worksheet **Resource 1.12: Fractured Fractions and Beyond** is designed to extend student understanding toward the development of algebraic representation. I would not overemphasize the variables. You will be surprised how the students will just use the variables, perhaps because there are choices available. The triangle area problem is a perfect example to use at this point. When fraction understanding is only algorithmic, students cannot "reconfigure" the algorithm to a nonconforming application. How many times have students looked at $\frac{1}{2}\cdot 11\cdot 10$ and gone through in order, rather than dividing the 10 by 2 then multiplying by the 11. One could argue that students also are troubled with this example: $4\times 15\times 25$, not noticing the 4×25 as the first choice for computing. If, in fact, your students miss this association component, take the time to develop this type of number sense with them.
Closure	The worksheet provided moves to an algorithmic platform. It would be appropriate to ask students where mistakes could be made. Error analysis is a teaching strategy that is often overlooked. Have students correct the homework in groups. Have each group submit a problem that students consider to be a novel way to answer the questions.

LESSON 1.4: PROBING COMPLEX FRACTIONS

Length: Three days

Unit Sequence	Teacher Reflections
Concepts C2, C9	
Principles P14, P15, P18, P19	
Skills S14	
Standards SD1, SD2, SD3, SD5, SD6, SD10, SD11, SD13	
Guiding Questions 1. How do the patterns generated by complex fractions compare to the patterns generated by simple fractions? 2. How can we use mental math to make complex fractions easy to understand?	
Background Information	The unit now combines equivalence and the rate concept through the use of a geometric model. This lesson also will develop relationships between the "improper" shaded fraction, the unshaded portion of that fraction, and the resulting values.
Introduction Pass out an index card to each student and invite them to find a partner. Ask each pair to work separately at first to write down what they think a complex fraction is. Once each student has completed the task, ask them to share with each other and compare definitions. Debrief the class to find out what students' perceptions and misperceptions about this term are.	This is an important task because it will reveal what students know and do not know about **complex fractions**, the topic for these lessons. Complex fractions are fractions that have a fraction in the numerator, denominator, or both. Many will not be familiar with the term. Others will confuse mixed numbers with complex fractions. Listen carefully for students' misconceptions when you debrief the class. If there are a number of misconceptions, make sure to write them down so that you can correct them as this lesson progresses.

Unit Sequence	Teacher Reflections

Teaching Strategies and Learning Experiences
 	
Days 1–3
 	
Move on to connecting complex fractions with rate of change. Use **Resource 1.14: Rectangle Pieces.**
 	
Teacher Note. A grid has not been included. Use graph paper. Each problem in Set A requires a separate graph. Students may want to assign different intervals for the independent axis and the dependent axis. (Use this vocabulary to promote advanced math thinking.)
 	
   Start the activity with Set A, modeling how to write complex fractions and graphing the rate of change for Sets 1–3. Make an overhead transparency to graph. Use one-inch blocks so that you can be accurate when graphing the fractional numerators. Use **Resource 1.14** with four sheets of graph paper. When graphing these, be quite demonstrative in your graphing. In Set A, Question 1, have the students go up $\frac{1}{2}$ a unit and over 1, then again up $\frac{1}{2}$ and over 1. Ask the students if there is an easier way to get to the second point. Be sure to write that if we do go up $\frac{1}{2}$ and over 1 twice, it is equivalent to going up 1 and over 2. Facilitate this discussion with the other sets: *do not* provide an algorithm (e.g., make equivalent fractions by multiplying numerator and denominator or complex fraction division). Students should do Question 4 independently.
 	
Guiding Questions. What fraction of each set is shaded? What fraction of the set is unshaded? Repeat the process for Set B. Add this question: Do I always have to graph this out to determine a rate of change with integers in the numerator and denominator?
 	
   Have the students graph $\frac{\frac{1}{2}}{1}$, repeating that "rise" and "run" three more times. Then make a connection between rise of $\frac{1}{2}$ and run of 1, as it compares to rise of 1 and run of 2. Repeat this throughout the activity: *do not* teach the complex fraction algorithm. This concept is crucial to understanding partial fractions in calculus.
	We are now connecting all the pieces for the students. It is important that the students go through the activities using the rate of change model that was used earlier in the unit. Students will start to make intuitive conversions, for example, $\frac{\frac{1}{2}}{1}$ will quickly turn into $\frac{1}{2}$. I have heard students say, "Well, if I move up $\frac{1}{2}$ a block and over 1 block you get to the point (1,2), which is $\frac{1}{2}$." They have similar connections to $\frac{\frac{1}{2}}{2}$: "This is easy, you just go up $\frac{1}{2}$ a block then over 2, which is really just $\frac{1}{2}$, and that is easy to see, because you can break up the rectangles into halves." When students have made this connection, the algorithm, while quite procedural, actually provides an answer that "makes sense" to the students.

Unit Sequence	Teacher Reflections
Have students complete Set C on their own, answering the following questions in writing: • What fraction of each set is shaded? • What fraction of each set is unshaded? • What is the rule you used for determining the shaded part? • What is the rule you used for determining the unshaded part? • If you combine the shaded and unshaded parts, what is the result? • What is the rate of change? **Resource 1.15: Rectangles Break Apart** can be additional independent or group work. It includes mental computation. By now, students should have developed an intuitive number sense of fractions through the use of partitioning and should be able to easily compute these problems mentally (without the need of an algorithm). **Resource 1.16: Rectangles on the Move** can be used as homework or as an assessment.	

Closure
 	
Administer **Resource 1.17: Post-Assessment: What Did You Learn About Fractions?** Compare pre-assessment and post-assessment results.
	Now is a good time to talk about the issues that arise with fractions. A fun activity is to create a fractions handbook. Have the students generate a list of common misconceptions, providing solutions that are modeled geometrically.
	    If you are in a school with younger students, have your class create a fractions packet for them. They could have cutout manipulatives for common fractions and word problems that can be modeled with the pieces.
	    Remember, you now have a group of students who have developed skill in modeling mathematical situations: *do not* let it end. Modeling is key to deep understanding.

SUGGESTED READINGS

American Association for the Advancement of Science. (1993). *Benchmarks for science literacy.* Washington, DC: Author.

Clarke, D. M., Roche A., & Mitchell, A. (2008). 10 practical tips for making fractions come alive and make sense. *Mathematics Teaching in the Middle School, 13*(7), 373–379.

Warrington, M. A. (1997). How children think about division with fractions. In D. L. Chambers (Ed.), *Putting research into practice in the elementary grades: Readings from Journals of the National Council of Teachers of Mathematics* (pp. 151–154). Reston, VA: National Council of Teachers of Mathematics.

RESOURCES

The following Resources can be found at the companion website for *Parallel Curriculum Units for Mathematics, Grades 6–12* at www.corwin.com/math6–12.

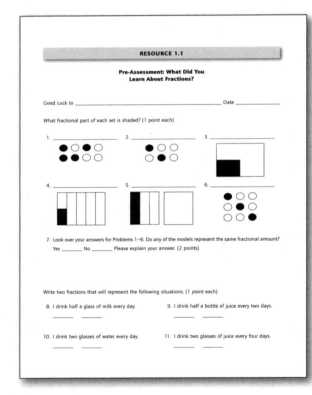

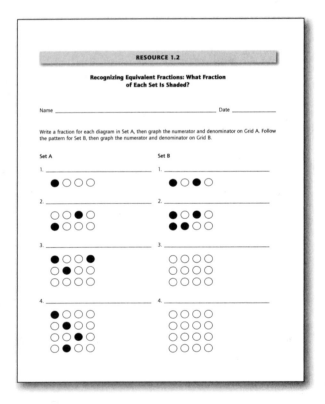

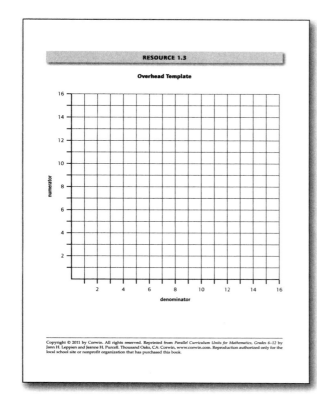

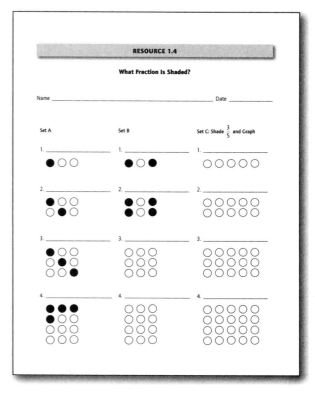

RESOURCE 1.3

Overhead Template

RESOURCE 1.4

What Fraction Is Shaded?

Name _____ Date _____

Set A   Set B   Set C: Shade $\frac{3}{5}$ and Graph

1. _____   1. _____   1. _____

2. _____   2. _____   2. _____

3. _____   3. _____   3. _____

4. _____   4. _____   4. _____

RESOURCE 1.5

Fractions and Rates of Change

Name _____ Date _____

Part I

What is the simplest way to represent this rate of change?

1. $\frac{3}{6} =$ _____   2. $\frac{3}{15} =$ _____   3. $\frac{35}{50} =$ _____

4. $\frac{27}{36} =$ _____   5. $\frac{12}{60} =$ _____   6. $\frac{7}{42} =$ _____

Part II

On each of the following four grids below, shade two-thirds of the rectangle strips to show equivalent fractions on each grid. Using a different color to represent each grid, plot your fractions on the graph and answer the questions below.

Grid 1

Grid 2

Grid 3

Grid 4

RESOURCE 1.6

Lemon Cookies

Name _____ Date _____

Here are some lemon cookies. Look at the cookies to find the answer to each question.

Example: Can you see thirds? How do you see them? How many cookies will you eat if you eat $\frac{2}{3}$ of the lemon cookies?

1. Can you see ninths? How do you see them? How many lemon cookies will you eat if you eat $\frac{4}{9}$ of the cookies?

2. Can you see sixths? How do you see them? How many lemon cookies will you eat if you eat $\frac{5}{6}$ of the cookies?

3. Can you see 36ths? How do you see them? How many lemon cookies will you eat if you eat $\frac{14}{36}$ of the cookies?

4. Can you see fourths? How do you see them? How many lemon cookies will you eat if you eat $\frac{3}{4}$ of the cookies?

5. Can you see 12ths? How do you see them? How many lemon cookies will you eat if you eat $\frac{5}{12}$ of the cookies?

RESOURCE 1.7

Our Favorites: Chocolate and Vanilla Cookies

Name _____ Date _____

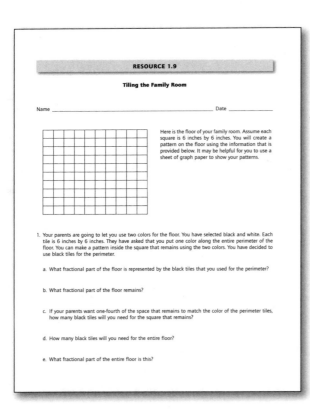

Here are some chocolate and vanilla cookies. Look at the cookies to find the answer to each question.

Example: If we put these cookies in six packs with an equal number of chocolate and vanilla cookies in each pack, how would you name the part of the cookies that is chocolate in each pack?

1. If we put the cookies in packs of four cookies each, what part of the cookies is chocolate?

2. If we wrap each cookie separately, how would you name the part of the cookies that is chocolate?

3. If we pack the cookies in dozens, how would you name the part of the cookies that is chocolate?

4. If we pack the cookies in packs of three cookies each, how would you name the part of the cookies that is chocolate?

5. The vanilla cookies fill four packages. Use packages of the same size to name the chocolate cookies.

6. The vanilla cookies fill $1\frac{1}{2}$ packages. Use packages of the same size to name the chocolate cookies.

7. The chocolate cookies fill $2\frac{2}{3}$ packages. Use packages of the same size to name the vanilla cookies.

RESOURCE 1.8

Cookies Template

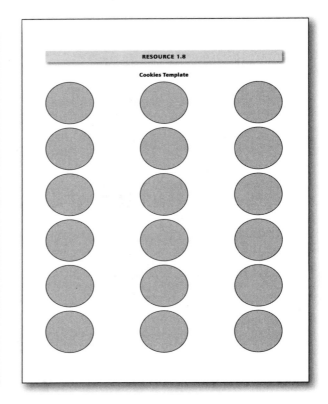

RESOURCE 1.9

Tiling the Family Room

Name _____ Date _____

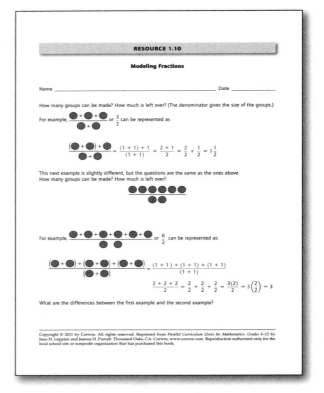

Here is the floor of your family room. Assume each square is 6 inches by 6 inches. You will create a pattern on the floor using the information that is provided below. It may be helpful for you to use a sheet of graph paper to show your patterns.

1. Your parents are going to let you use two colors for the floor. You have selected black and white. Each tile is 6 inches by 6 inches. They have asked that you put one color along the entire perimeter of the floor. You can make a pattern inside the square that remains using the two colors. You have decided to use black tiles for the perimeter.

    a. What fractional part of the floor is represented by the black tiles that you used for the perimeter?

    b. What fractional part of the floor remains?

    c. If your parents want one-fourth of the space that remains to match the color of the perimeter tiles, how many black tiles will you need for the square that remains?

    d. How many black tiles will you need for the entire floor?

    e. What fractional part of the entire floor is this?

RESOURCE 1.10

Modeling Fractions

Name _____ Date _____

How many groups can be made? How much is left over? (The denominator gives the size of the groups.)

For example, $\dfrac{(\bullet + \bullet) + \bullet}{\bullet + \bullet}$ or $\dfrac{3}{2}$ can be represented as

$$\frac{(\bullet + \bullet) + \bullet}{(\bullet + \bullet)} = \frac{(1 + 1) + 1}{(1 + 1)} = \frac{2 + 1}{2} = \frac{2}{2} + \frac{1}{2} = 1\frac{1}{2}$$

This next example is slightly different, but the questions are the same as the ones above. How many groups can be made? How much is left over?

For example, $\dfrac{\bullet + \bullet + \bullet + \bullet + \bullet + \bullet}{\bullet + \bullet}$ or $\dfrac{6}{2}$ can be represented as:

$$\frac{(\bullet + \bullet) + (\bullet + \bullet) + (\bullet + \bullet)}{(\bullet + \bullet)} = \frac{(1 + 1) + (1 + 1) + (1 + 1)}{(1 + 1)}$$

$$\frac{2 + 2 + 2}{2} = \frac{2}{2} + \frac{2}{2} + \frac{2}{2} = \frac{3(2)}{2} = 3\left(\frac{2}{2}\right) = 3$$

What are the differences between the first example and the second example?

RESOURCE 1.11

Working With Fractions

Name _____ Date _____

1. Use the methods just modeled to show the steps that will lead from the geometric model to the numerical representation.

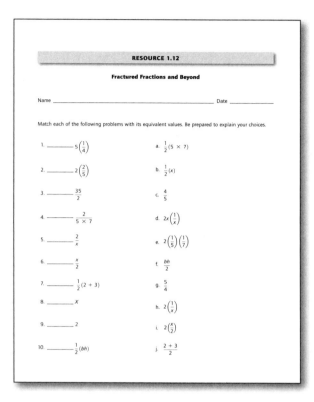

a.

b.

c.

d.

2. Using what you discovered above, write the following fractions as mixed numbers in simplified form.

a. $\frac{5}{3} =$ b. $\frac{2+6}{2+3} =$ c. $\frac{2+(3+3)}{2+(3+2)} =$ d. $\frac{8}{5} =$

e. $\frac{2+(3\cdot2)}{2+(3\cdot1)} =$ f. $\frac{12}{10} =$ g. $\frac{2\cdot6}{2\cdot5} =$ h. $\frac{8}{7} =$

i. $\frac{2\cdot5}{2\cdot3} =$ j. $\frac{2+6}{2+5} =$ k. $\frac{2\cdot(3+3)}{2\cdot(3+2)} =$ l. $\frac{1+4}{1+2} =$

RESOURCE 1.12

Fractured Fractions and Beyond

Name _____ Date _____

Match each of the following problems with its equivalent values. Be prepared to explain your choices.

1. _____ $5\left(\frac{1}{4}\right)$ a. $\frac{1}{2}(5 \times 7)$

2. _____ $2\left(\frac{2}{5}\right)$ b. $\frac{1}{2}(x)$

3. _____ $\frac{35}{2}$ c. $\frac{4}{5}$

4. _____ $\frac{2}{5 \times 7}$ d. $2x\left(\frac{1}{x}\right)$

5. _____ $\frac{2}{x}$ e. $2\left(\frac{1}{5}\right)\left(\frac{1}{7}\right)$

6. _____ $\frac{x}{2}$ f. $\frac{bh}{2}$

7. _____ $\frac{1}{2}(2+3)$ g. $\frac{5}{4}$

8. _____ x h. $2\left(\frac{1}{x}\right)$

9. _____ 2 i. $2\left(\frac{x}{2}\right)$

10. _____ $\frac{1}{2}(bh)$ j. $\frac{2+3}{2}$

RESOURCE 1.13

Decomposing Fractions

Name _____ Date _____

Decompose the following problems by giving two alternative forms that will result in the same numerical answer. If you can simplify the fraction, then simplify it.

1. $\frac{5}{8} =$ _____ = _____   Simplify = _____

2. $\frac{2+4}{3+4} =$ _____ = _____   Simplify = _____

3. $\frac{3(1+1)}{2(1+3)} =$ _____ = _____   Simplify = _____

4. $\frac{2}{5}(10) =$ _____ = _____   Simplify = _____

5. $\frac{2}{5}\left(\frac{1}{10}\right) =$ _____ = _____   Simplify = _____

6. $\frac{1}{3}(12r^2) =$ _____ = _____   Simplify = _____

7. $(4+3)\left(\frac{x}{7}\right) =$ _____ = _____   Simplify = _____

Write the following fractions as mixed numbers in simplified form.

8. $\frac{7}{3} =$ _____   9. $\frac{3+6}{3+3} =$ _____

10. $\frac{4+(6+6)}{4+(6+4)} =$ _____   11. $\frac{9}{7} =$ _____

12. $\frac{4+(6\times4)}{4+(6\times2)} =$ _____   13. $\frac{8}{6} =$ _____

14. $\frac{4\times6}{4\times5} =$ _____   15. $\frac{3}{2} =$ _____

16. $\frac{2\times4}{2\times3} =$ _____   17. $\frac{2+6}{2+5} =$ _____

18. $\frac{2\times(3+3)}{2\times(3+2)} =$ _____   19. $\frac{1+4}{1+2} =$ _____

RESOURCE 1.14

Rectangle Pieces

Name _____ Date _____

Set A

1. ▪☐

2. ▪☐☐

3. ▪☐☐☐

4. ▪☐☐☐☐

Number of Blocks	Shaded Part as a Complex Fraction	Simple Form for the Shaded Part	Unshaded Part as a Complex Fraction	Simple Form for the Unshaded Part	Sum of the Simple Shaded and the Simple Unshaded
1					
2					
3					
4					

Set B

1. ▪☐

2. ▪☐☐

3. ▪☐☐☐

4. ▪☐☐☐☐

Number of Blocks	Shaded Part as a Complex Fraction	Simple Form for the Shaded Part	Unshaded Part as a Complex Fraction	Simple Form for the Unshaded Part	Sum of the Simple Shaded and the Simple Unshaded
1					
2					
3					
4					

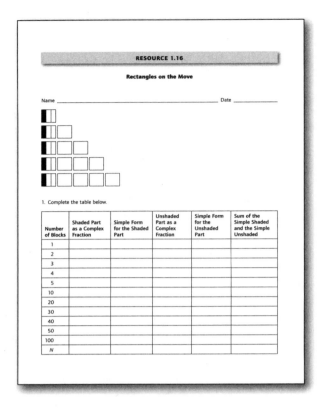

RESOURCE 1.15

Rectangles Break Apart

Name _____ Date _____

1. Complete the table below.

Number of Blocks	Shaded Part as a Complex Fraction	Simple Form for the Shaded Part	Unshaded Part as a Complex Fraction	Simple Form for the Unshaded Part	Sum of the Simple Shaded and the Simple Unshaded
1					
2					
3					
4					
5					
10					
20					
30					
40					
50					
100					

RESOURCE 1.16

Rectangles on the Move

Name _____ Date _____

1. Complete the table below.

Number of Blocks	Shaded Part as a Complex Fraction	Simple Form for the Shaded Part	Unshaded Part as a Complex Fraction	Simple Form for the Unshaded Part	Sum of the Simple Shaded and the Simple Unshaded
1					
2					
3					
4					
5					
10					
20					
30					
40					
50					
100					
N					

RESOURCE 1.17

Post-Assessment:
What Did You Learn About Fractions?

Good Luck to _____ Date _____

What fractional part of each set is shaded? (1 point each)

1. _____   2. _____   3. _____

4. _____   5. _____   6. _____

7. Look over your answers for Problems 1–6. Do any of the models represent the same fractional amount?

Yes _____ No _____ Please explain your answer. (2 points)

Write two fractions that will represent the following situations. (1 point each)

8. I drink half a glass of milk every day.   9. I drink half a bottle of juice every two days.
_____ _____   _____ _____

10. I drink two glasses of water every day.   11. I drink two glasses of juice every four days.
_____ _____   _____ _____

2

Linear Programming

A Key to Decision Making, Grades 9–10

Marianne Cavanaugh

INTRODUCTION TO THE UNIT

The development of linear programming is a basic topic in algebra and is of fundamental importance in advanced mathematics. Linear programming is a mathematical procedure for solving systems of linear equations for common solutions. As such, creating, interpreting, and working with an algebraic rule for a linear function are not trivial tasks: they are the foundation for all of algebra. Students can transfer many of the important concepts learned through the study of linear functions to the understanding of other functions. Many of the problems encountered in calculus are grounded in real-world situations.

According to the National Council of Teachers of Mathematics (NCTM; 2000, p. 223), "It is essential that [students] become comfortable in relating symbolic expressions containing variables to verbal, tabular, and graphical representations of numerical and quantitative relationships. Students should develop an initial understanding of several different meanings and uses of variables through representing quantities in a variety of problem situations." The study of linear functions provides students with their first experience in identifying and interpreting the relationship between two dependent variables. Although linear equations are the simplest equations that students encounter, they are not the easiest to learn.

Linear equations are the first opportunity for students to practice operating with equations and to develop equation-solving skills. Students are at a significant crossroads in their mathematical development when they encounter these ideas. It is the point at which many of them make a decision about their future as mathematicians and as consumers who will use mathematics to make informed decisions.

Having the opportunity to experience a concrete functional approach can make the difference in the students' mathematical self-efficacy. This foundational unit is designed to enhance student confidence and lay the foundation for future successful experiences in algebra.

Linear functions are easily accessible functions to study from a modeling or functional approach. Additionally, linear functions can be one of the most intuitive equations to solve when real-world applications provide the avenue for the solving process. In providing a strong foundation built on sequential concrete experiences with linear functions and programming, we provide the opportunity for enhanced mathematical understanding in upper-level math. One of the key ideas of differential calculus (finding the slope of the tangent line) is to approximate more-complicated functions using linear functions, and then to calculate with the linear functions, ultimately using those answers to study the more-complicated functions.

Students should be able to move fluidly between the different representations of linear functions and, given a description of a situation, should be able to produce an equation, table, and graph. Likewise, when given an algebraic representation for a linear function, students should be able to produce the others. To do this, they need ample opportunities to explore situations involving linear functions in all representations.

When studying linear functions graphically, students gain an understanding that the slope of the line represents a constant rate of change for the function, and that the y-intercept is the point where the graph crosses the y-axis and often represents the initial condition or starting point for the function. Through practical experience of solving linear function problems in context, students develop an understanding of the concepts and real-world meanings of the slopes and y-intercepts of lines.

Inherent in the development of the linear functions and the linear programming activities is the attention to different types of data. It important to distinguish between data that are represented as a set of discrete points versus data that are continuous. This distinction is extremely important as students move ahead in upper-level mathematics. Within those areas of discussion, domain and range of a function emerge. Students need to understand that some models are limited due to constraints within the problem.

It is challenging for students to identify the structure for two seemingly unrelated variables. To create or interpret such a relationship requires deeper understanding on the part of the learner. The notion that the dependent variable will depend on the independent variable indicates a shift to higher-order thinking. Additionally, students need to see that there are many conventions inherent in linear functions: variable choices, implicit operators (multiplication), initial value (y-intercept), rate of change (coefficient of the variable—not just "x"), and the relationship of the graph to the real world.

Graphing real-world data provides opportunities for students to predict outcomes with reasonable certainty. Outcomes couched in solid mathematical understanding that take into consideration concepts such as domain, range, continuous versus discrete data, and outliers are critical. If students can interpret trend data, they can use that information to make informed decisions.

Linear functions and their use in determining common solutions for problems with numerous constraints are foundational to upper-level math. This introductory unit provides a solid foundation for students. It is designed to open the doors for all students as mathematicians to meet the NCTM mandate to develop algebraic thinking in all students. It provides the building blocks that will empower the acquisition of advanced mathematical topics in a structured, layered approach.

How Are the Lessons Different From Others?

These lessons differ from more-traditional units in three ways. First, they are constructivist, they address student misconceptions, and they illustrate real-world applications of linear programming. Although our focus is developmental math, this module should provide a smooth transition to the rigors of a typical algebra course, providing the scaffolded development necessary for success. Students actively participate in both mental and physical exploration of point placement, the relationship between points and linear graphs, and the interpretation of slope. Students completing the module can expect to have gained an appreciation of linear functions as a useful tool that can be applied to real-life situations.

Research confirms that beginning algebra students use various intuitive methods for solving algebraic equations. Some of these methods may help their understanding of equations and equation solving. By contrast, students who are taught to solve equations by formal methods may not understand what they are doing. Students who are taught to use the method of "transposing" are found to only mechanically apply the "change side–change sign" rule.

Second, these activities are designed to "take advantage" of students' intuitive methods, and this is the second difference between traditional lessons and those included here. The lessons address the following misconceptions that result from the traditional, formal approach to instruction:

- Interpreting graphs of situations as literal pictures rather than as symbolic representations of situations (Leinhardt, Zaslavsky, & Stein 1990)
- Confounding the slope of a graph with the maximum or the minimum value and failing to realize that the slope of a graph is a measure of rate (Clement, 1989)
- Having difficulties with the notions of interval scale and coordinates when constructing graphs (Leinhardt, Zaslavsky, & Stein, 1990; Vergnaud & Errecalde, 1980; Wavering, 1985)
- Reading graphs point by point, and ignoring their global features
- Having difficulty translating between graphical and algebraic representations, especially when moving from a graph into an equation (Leinhardt et al., 1990)

The goal is to highlight the practical role that linear programming plays in our world; this is the third way these lessons differ from traditional approaches. Problems that are familiar to students are modeled and implicitly linked to algebraic representations and the resulting graphic model. Many students may shrug their shoulders and say, "Why do we need to know this?" The goal of this unit is to demonstrate how "linear functions are useful in students' everyday lives." For example, a person can study a relationship between the number of minutes used and the cost on a cell phone bill. Linear functions can model the relationship between pounds of hamburger needed for the school picnic if everyone eats two quarter-pounders. Linear programming can help you make a decision about a part-time job with an hourly rate and one with a flat rate plus commission. The focus on real-life examples enables students to take the concepts of linear functions out of the classroom and into their everyday lives.

In addition, a functional approach to linear functions is a key strategy, which means that there is no formal teaching of definitions of function and domain.

Without fanfare, the notation is simply used in presenting the lesson, and the focus is on developing an understanding of the relationship between the independent and the dependent variables. This methodology has been deliberately selected; its use has been designed to enhance an intuitive understanding of variable and structure, and the interpretation of functions and their graphs.

Finally, the unit provides a solid foundation for students' future success in higher-level math. It is designed to open the doors for all students as mathematicians and to meet the NCTM mandate for developing algebraic thinking in all students.

CONTENT FRAMEWORK

Discipline-Specific Concepts

C1: Algebraic modeling

C2: Limits

C3: Discrete data

C4: Continuity

C5: Domain and the independent variable

C6: Constraints

C7: Range and the dependent variable

C8: Slope/coefficient relationship

C9: Linear function

C10: Parallel relationships

C11: Perpendicular relationships

C12: Intercepts

C13: Rate of change

C14: Outliers

C15: Direct variation

C16: Line of best fit/linear regression

Principles and Generalizations

P1: A linear function describes a relationship.

P2: A linear function can model positive real-world relationships—for example, earning a fixed amount of money over time.

P3: A linear function can model negative real-world relationships—for example, spending a fixed amount of money on lunch every day.

P4: Skill in modeling real-world data with an appropriate linear model will result in informed decision making.

P5: Graphs are mathematical models that can represent real-world relationships.

P6: A graph can model a linear function.

P7: A table of values can be generated from a linear function.

P8: The table of values for a linear relationship is an example of direct variation.

P9: Continuity is important in modeling real-world data. Some functions are continuous, such as accelerating as you drive a car, while others are not continuous, such as rising postal rates.

P10: Domain and range are constraints that have an effect on the linear model.

P11: Linear programming provides a strategy to find common solutions.

P12: Linear relationships can represent change.

P13: The type of change in a linear relationship can be determined by the coefficient linked to the variable.

P14: The graph of linear function can model the rate of change in a relationship.

P15: Some linear systems may not have a common solution that can be used to answer a real-world problem.

P16: There can be linear systems that will never have a solution; the relationship among the elements in the linear system may represent a system of equivalent rates of change resulting in parallel relationships.

P17: Some relationships "appear" linear, but they can be modeled only by an approximation of a linear function.

P18: If real-world data can be modeled using a line of best fit, you can make a prediction about the data.

P19: Some real-world problems have limits; you need to take that into consideration when making predictions.

P20: Linear functions are important for providing a first experience in identifying and interpreting the relationship between two dependent variables.

P21: Linear functions provide connections to the real world.

National Mathematics Standards

SD1: Generalize patterns using explicitly defined linear functions.

SD2: Understand relations and functions; and select, convert flexibly among, and use various representations for those relations and functions.

SD3: Analyze linear functions of one variable by investigating rates of change and intercepts.

SD4: Understand and perform transformations such as arithmetically combining and composing commonly used functions.

SD5: Understand and compare the properties of classes of linear functions.

SD6: Interpret representations of functions of two variables, including parallel and perpendicular.

SD7: Use symbolic algebra to represent and explain real-world relationships.

SD8: Identify essential quantitative relationships in a situation and determine the equation or system of equations that might model the relationships.

SD9: Draw reasonable conclusions about a linear function being modeled.

SD10: Develop and evaluate inferences and predictions that are based on data from a linear system.

SD11: Understand scatter plots and use them to model trend behavior.

SD12: Apply and adapt a variety of appropriate strategies to solve problems, using equations, tables, and graphs.

SD13: Monitor and reflect on the process of linear functions and programming as a problem-solving process.

SD14: Use reasoning as a fundamental aspect in interpreting linear models.

SD15: Understand how equations, tables, and graphs interconnect to build on one another to produce a coherent whole.

Skills

S1: Write equivalent forms of equations and systems of equations and solve them with fluency—mentally or with paper and pencil in simple cases.

S2: Judge the meaning, utility, and reasonableness of a prediction or estimation using a linear model.

S3: Use an algebraic equation to represent relationships arising from various contexts.

S4: Approximate and interpret rates of change from graphical and numerical data.

S5: Formulate questions that can be addressed with data from linear relationships, then collect, organize, and display relevant data to answer those questions.

S6: Use scatter plots to display data.

S7: Use a line of best fit, when appropriate, to reason and predict.

S8: Create and use algebraic linear representations to organize, record, and communicate mathematical ideas to peers, teachers, and others.

S9: Use the language of mathematics (domain, range, continuity, discrete, slope) to precisely express the concepts of linear functions and programming.

S10: Use, apply, and translate mathematical representations (tables, linear models, graphs) to model and interpret mathematical phenomena in order to solve problems.

S11: Plot points to create a linear model in Quadrant I.

S12: Find coordinate solutions.

S13: Choose table values utilizing knowledge about factors and multiples when working with fractional coefficients.

S14: Compute with fractional rates of change.

Guiding Questions That Students Will Answer as They Complete the Lessons

Core Curriculum

1. What is a linear function and what does it tell us about the real-world situation it represents?

2. How can we use a linear function to make predictions and estimations?

3. How does the coefficient of the variable provide information about the model?

4. What is the real-world interpretation for the y-intercept?

5. How can you represent real-world data using an algebraic model?

6. How can a mathematical model like a graph help us understand data?

7. How does the algebraic or mathematical model tell you what is happening with your data?

8. How can you use more than one rule to describe data?

9. What characteristics of our algebraic model enable us to determine whether a common solution can be found?

10. How does a graph help you determine the reasonableness of your answer?

11. How are linear functions useful?

Curriculum of Practice

1. How do practitioners organize their knowledge and skills in mathematics?

2. What strategies does the practitioner use to solve routine and nonroutine problems in mathematics?

3. What tools does a mathematician use to communicate her understandings?

4. On what basis does a practitioner in the field draw answers and conclusions?

5. What makes some real-world data continuous and other data discrete?

6. When would you have a limit for a real-world model?

7. Can we always (or, Why is it not possible to) find a common solution to a real-world problem?

8. When is it appropriate to use a fractional rate in a real-world model?

ASSESSMENTS

This chapter, **Linear Programming: A Key to Decision Making, Grades 9–10**, contains a matched pre- and post-assessment. The 10 items on the assessments have been purposefully created to assess important concepts, skills, and understandings. Item 1 should be prior knowledge for all students: it requires them to understand one-to-one correspondence and the representation of numbers on a graph. Item 2 also should be familiar to students. Students are required to plot points on a graph correctly using real-world data. Item 3 assesses students' knowledge of continuous functions, unlike the discrete points they graphed in Item 1 and Item 2. Item 4 requires a deeper understanding of continuous functions because it challenges students to plot at a different point on the y-axis. Instead of starting their plot at 0, students are asked to begin at 100. This item also requires a student to understand that graphs can be partitioned into different intervals, such as 5, 10, and 50. Items 5 and 6 are companion items. In Item 5, students are asked to graph a continuous, increasing function, whereas in Item 6, students are asked to graph a continuous but decreasing function. Item 7, a multiple-step problem, requires students to put their data from Items 5 and 6 onto a single graph. It is an optimization problem that uses linear relationships, the primary focus of calculus. Item 8 requires a shift to abstract thinking. As such, teachers can use student work on this problem as an indicator of student readiness for working with linear functions. Items 9 and 10 may be perplexing to most students when they see them for the first time: Item 9 has no solution and students are unaccustomed to seeing these kinds of equations. The solution for Item 10 includes perpendicular lines, another phenomenon seldom seen by students.

It is important for teachers to use these 10 items to gauge not only their students' prior knowledge, but also their growth across the lessons. Pre-assessment data will help teachers pinpoint where they need to begin their instruction. The data from the post-assessment will assist the teacher to determine how well the students mastered the concepts, skills, and understandings in the lessons. Ongoing formative assessments—such as homework and class discussions—will help the teacher to differentiate instruction around the learning needs of subgroups of students.

Many suggestions for differentiation are incorporated into these lessons. These suggestions are based on many years of experience with middle and high school mathematics students. The following reflections about above-grade-level learners, on-grade-level learners, and below-grade-level learners should be coupled with the reader's knowledge of his or her students.

UNIT SEQUENCE, DESCRIPTION, AND TEACHER REFLECTIONS

Of primary importance in mathematics is the notion that relationships in the real world can be modeled using a graph, which is a linear model. The development of deep understanding in this area underpins the development of skills that are required in algebra. Modeling starts with a problem that needs a solution, the goal being to find the best solution within a given set of constraints. Skill development in modeling emerges when students have multiple, ongoing opportunities to engage with contextual situations that make sense to them and that support the dual mathematical goals of developing the symbolic representation of the situation and being able to translate the symbolic representation to the verbal.

It can be said that Algebra 1 is essentially the development of equation-solving skills and the application of those skills to model real-world applications. This unit is designed to provide educational opportunities for students to engage in this worthwhile mathematical endeavor. This foundational curriculum unit provides linked activities that lead students to preliminary understandings in these areas. The activities are accessible to many levels of students and provide the opportunity to reengage students in the math class.

Inherent in the linear functions and the linear programming activities is the attention to different types of data. It important to distinguish between data that are represented as a set of discrete points versus data that are continuous. These issues are extremely important as students move ahead in upper-level mathematics. Within those areas of discussion, domain and range of a function emerge. Students need to understand that some models are limited, due to constraints within the problem.

Additionally, this notion of graphing real-world data provides opportunities for students to predict outcomes with reasonable certainty. Outcomes couched in solid mathematical understanding that takes into consideration concepts such as domain, range, continuous versus discrete data, and outliers are critical. If a student can interpret trend data, she can use that information to make informed decisions.

Finally, skill and success in the use of linear equations and in linear programming can provide options for the student to move ahead mathematically. In using the mathematics terminology and methods that are used extensively in Algebra 1 and Algebra 2, teachers can empower students. Developing student self-efficacy in mathematical problem solving has numerous benefits, the least of which is that success breeds success. This introductory unit seeks to meet many of the challenges inherent in Algebra 1 and 2.

It is important to note that assessments (**Resource 2.1: Pre-Assessment: What Do You Know About Word Problems and Functions?** and **Resource 2.17: Post-Assessment: What Do You Know About Word Problems and Functions?**) are included with this unit. The pre-assessment is included at the end of Lesson 2.1 and again at the conclusion of Lesson 2.3. Teachers should plan to administer the pre-assessment at least two weeks prior to the actual start of these lessons. Once administered and once data have been collected about students' prior knowledge levels, teachers can adjust their instruction, plan for flexible small groups—if significant differences among students appear—and gather the necessary resources. The pre- and post-assessment are aligned, thereby providing teachers with the opportunity to measure student growth.

LESSON 2.1: LINEAR PROGRAMMING ESSENTIALS: CONTINUITY, DOMAIN, AND RANGE

Length: Four days

Unit Sequence	Teacher Reflections
Concepts C1, C2, C3, C4, C5, C6, C7, C8, C13, C15	Some of the issues that perplex students in calculus—e.g., continuity, domain, and range—are significant issues. Students' failures to note the importance of continuity, domain, and range contribute to numerous misinterpretations and serious errors. Success in higher-level math is dependent on a solid foundation, which is built only if students have the opportunity to explore the application of significant mathematical concepts in the context of real-world applications. Quite often, we move to graphing linear functions from a rather algorithmic approach using linear equations, and we dismiss real-world applications as being too time-consuming, and as too much of an interference with the "real mathematics." It is important to remember that almost all of the problems that we attempt to solve in calculus are grounded in real-world situations. By developing skill in modeling real-world data and taking into consideration the issues of continuity, domain, and range, students can develop the necessary problem-solving skills that will enable them to evaluate data resulting in informed decision making. By observing a data model, students will develop their ability to predict outcomes. It is the skill of interpreting the mathematical model as a representation of a qualitative experience that allows students to answer the age-old question: "When are we ever going to use this?" with the answer, "Every day."
Principles P1, P2, P3, P4, P5, P7, P9, P10, P11, P12, P14, P19, P20	
Skills S1, S2, S3, S4, S5, S9, S10, S11, S12	
Standards SD1, SD3, SD7, SD8, SD9, SD10, SD12, SD14, SD15	

Unit Sequence	Teacher Reflections
Guiding Question(s) 1. How can you represent real-world data using an algebraic model? 2. How does the model tell you what is happening with your data? 3. What makes some real-world data continuous and other data discrete? 4. When would you have a limit for a real-world model? 5. How can you use more than one rule to describe data?	

Introduction
 	
Lesson 2.1 consists of a series of scaffolded lessons that introduce students to the concepts that underlay linear programming and use student-centered, fun problems. The problems within each lesson build on one another in a way that allows the teacher to introduce the concepts and corresponding mathematical vocabulary in a natural way.
 	
To hook students' interest, introduce the unit by posing questions similar to the following:
 	
• If you know how much you earn every week babysitting, can you predict how much you will have in two months?
• If you are saving for an iPod, can you determine how long it will take you to save enough money?
• Have you been involved in making a decision about cell phone plans from different companies?
• Do you have to pay for text messaging? If so, which plan is the cheapest for you?
• Have you ever made plans to meet up with friends who are traveling from a different part of town?
• If you try to meet your friends at the mall, how do you decide on a time and how do you know you can get there in time?
	The following is a recommendation for the entire unit: I find that making transparencies for most worksheets is particularly helpful, for both teachers and students. When using the transparencies, you provide accurate visual representations for your students. Additionally, students can create the "answer sheets" and then present their results to the class. In making these presentations, you can ensure the correct use of terminology and procedures. This is particularly helpful for students who require numerous avenues for content acquisition.
	   Students quickly see the connection between linear programming and their own lives when these types of questions are posed. As you are asking the questions, it is important to discuss with the students how determining relationships and finding a common solution based on facts would enable them to make an informed decision. Have students generate a few solutions of their own.
	   The mathematical connection is strengthened if you sketch linear models as each question is raised: a dotted line to show babysitting earnings; another dotted line to show saved money; and a system to show cell phone plans. It increases the challenge for a range of students if the discussion includes the unexpected, such as a line for saving money that flattens out and asking the class what they think happened to the savings plan.
	   This direct connection of their personal experiences with concrete connections to the mathematical model that represents those experiences provides the anchor and the motivation for students as you move forward with this unit.

Unit Sequence	Teacher Reflections

Teaching Strategies and Learning Experiences
 	
Day 1
 	
The purpose of this lesson is to help students understand that tables, graphs, symbols, and verbal explanations are alternative ways of representing the same data and relationships, and to help students become skilled in translating from one representation to another.
    Resource 2.2: Graphing Real-World Data is a whole-class activity.
    It is imperative to lead students through Problems 1 and 2 with rich discussions, suggestions for which follow.
    Problem 1 is designed to introduce the notion of discrete points. This is not a continuous function. In fact, you need to "jump" from one data point to another. This is known as "jump discontinuity" in calculus. In addressing this jumping, spend time discussing exactly how you move in order to jump to the next point—that is, make sure that the notion for rate of change (slope) is clear, with discrete points.
    You also will need to discuss the domain (Is this a problem with an infinite number of students?) and range (How many students can reasonably fit in your classroom?). Is there a limit to the answers? How does the domain relate to the range?
    In this case, the domain and range will be the same. The relationship has major ramifications in advanced math and a topic you will continue to develop in greater depth as the unit continues.
    Discussion also should be conducted on why the grid is set up the way it is. Why is Quadrant I the only quadrant for the data? This should be tied into the domain/range discussion as well. Also, do not forget to talk about the origin as the starting point for the data.
    You should also spend time creating the algebraic representation for the students.
    Problem 2, on the other hand, is continuous. Spend time discussing many of the same concepts from Problem 1, including continuity, comparing and contrasting continuity with the first problem. Slope can take on another dimension here: what about starting at $x = \frac{1}{2}$? Is the up and over the same?
	Day 1
	
	Use a transparency for **Resource 2.2: Graphing Real-World Data** to provide the visual component that is crucial for most students. Using the transparency allows you to have students who finish early put their solutions on the transparency as you spend time helping those students who may need support.
	    I always find it interesting to do this lesson with students; invariably every student connects the points to make a line. Students seldom see data that are discrete, since the motivation for most units on linear programming goes directly from the linear equation to the linear system. Likewise, teachers, in my experience, rush to the linear function continuous model.
	    Spend time discussing this issue. You can have students give examples of other situations that have discrete data points. This discussion will help set the stage for Problems 5 and 6. When reproducing the worksheets, Problems 5 and 6 should be single-sided so that student work can be posted.
	
	    If you have students who are advanced, you can move them to a standard form, $f(x) = mx + b$. If you do, please note that function notation is used. The concept of function is very important and there is no reason not to introduce it.

Unit Sequence	Teacher Reflections
Problem 4 can present issues for students in the assignment of the independent (minutes) and dependent (gallons) variables. Be sure to talk about direct variation when you work on these activities. For Problems 5 and 6, students post their solutions. With the class, decide on those solutions that are most interesting.	After thorough discussions regarding Problems 1 and 2, students should be able to complete Problem 3 independently. Take the time to verify that all students are able to provide an algebraic model; have students put their answers on the transparency. Now is a very good time to explain why time is independent. Whether you fill the pool or not, time is still passing by. This understanding is crucial for advanced mathematical problem solving. The scenarios are realistic, so students should be able to incorporate the concept with little or no hesitation. Through discussions and resolution of misconceptions that surface when working with **Resource 2.2: Graphing Real-World Data**, students are able to take control of their learning—to solve problems that are "new" but predicated on classroom discourse.
Closure **Resource 2.3: Interesting Developments in Data** is designed to be a homework sheet, reinforcing the skills, concepts, and discussions that were developed during the lessons. Additionally, it provides opportunities for students to work with negative slope, laying the foundation for the next day's lesson.	

Day 2
 	
Use **Resource 2.4: Up and Down the Mountain: Will We Ever Meet?** as a class activity. This lesson is designed to demonstrate that problems can be solved by modeling the use of two equations that are equal to one another and by solving algebraically.
    Start with an explicit discussion of negative and positive slope by referring to Problem 5 from the previous night's homework.
    The motivation for today's lesson should come from the last problem in the homework. This activity should develop rather quickly.
	Expect students to come to class telling you that some of the problems that they did "went down" and wondering if they were correct. Engaging in a discussion at this point provides true mathematical discourse. Students can be quite articulate in their explanations, often using nonmathematical terms. It is imperative that you interject appropriate math vocabulary as they defend their answers. In the long run, the appropriate use of vocabulary provides the foundation for accurate mathematical understanding and makes upper-level math more accessible.
	    Resource 2.4: Up and Down the Mountain: Will We Ever Meet? will use the graph model to find a common solution to a real-world problem. The points of intersection can be determined from the graphs.
	    Depending on the group, you can introduce the notion of the feasible region and how the points in that region are all "solutions" to the problem as an enrichment topic that can be used to differentiate for above-grade-level students. This topic will require the extension to inequalities and graphing inequalities on the coordinate plane.

Unit Sequence	Teacher Reflections
In Problem 1, establish a positive slope and an algebraic expression with appropriate variables. If there is discussion about "discrete and continuous," address that issue at this point. Move right along to Problem 2, linking it to the last problem from the homework. Discussion about the consequences of using different intervals for each axis is well warranted. Students will need guidance in the verification process. Now move on to the final component for this problem, "When will Shontrell and Fayed meet?" This will involve some discussion about common factors for the independent and dependent axes. Students can work independently or in small groups to complete Problems 4, 5, and 6. In Problem 4, they are establishing a y-intercept different from the origin.	Problems 1 and 2 represent similar situations. Now is the time to discuss the one cookie with five chips relationship with the two cookies and ten chips relationship: this is an opportunity to talk about various ways to model and convey information. Talk about slope. Have the students compare the slope for Problem 1 with the slope for Problem 2. There will be interesting discussions concerning Problem 5, since the first point is $(0,10)$. Some students will start at $(1,10)$. This homework problem develops the notion of a y-intercept other than $(0,0)$. Discussion about the y-intercept is crucial: this is often the stumbling point in developing the equation. Resolving that problem can be done in the space provided on the worksheet. One of the major issues for students will be establishing appropriate units for the two situations. This is an appropriate time to show that you have solved the problem by modeling and that you can solve the problem by setting the two equations equal to one another and then by solving algebraically. Your students may need help in establishing this equation, though they should be able to connect it to Problem 2.
Closure **Resource 2.5: My Models and Graphs** can be used for class or homework. This is the time for students to summarize the same data using an algebraic model and a graph, and to create a word problem that will mirror the model.	
Day 3 Make sure that you review student work from this worksheet on Day 3. The problems on this sheet do not have a real-world application and can be extended to form lines. Talk about why this is true. Depending on the level of the student, integers would be good to introduce at this time.	**Resource 2.5: My Models and Graphs** is provided as a more routine practice set with an integration to real-world connections as opposed to traditionally assigned "plot and graph" problems. I always find it interesting to see who has the clever situations. These kinds of creative opportunities provide a lens for measuring algebraic understanding in a nontraditional way. Some of you may question my decision to ask for five points. In my

Unit Sequence	Teacher Reflections
	opinion, student skills are quite weak in basic computation. This is my way of getting in the drill and practice in a palatable fashion. I would also allow the use of a scientific calculator if necessary. There are opportunities for the graphing calculator later.
Closure *Days 3 and 4* **Resource 2.6: The Match Game: Problems, Graphs, and Models** is a nontraditional formative assessment. Use index cards and have students create a matching game that includes three components: an equation, a matching word problem, and a matching graph. As students are creating the game cards, walk around the room monitoring progress and checking for student understanding. This assessment will take more than a single day. Creating the game may very well take an entire period and the peer assessment component could take another day. Encourage students to be creative. After the games are created, use **Resource 2.7: Peer Assessment Scoring Rubric.** You can cut these up and distribute as many sheets as games you want played.	*Days 3 and 4* Assessments that students create are very powerful. The teacher's main task is to be as clear as possible on the scoring rubric. The included rubric came after numerous trials and student questions, so don't become discouraged when you venture on your own to create a rubric that provides the information you are truly seeking. Provide zip-top baggies to store the game sets. The game bags are then "played" by other groups of students, who verify the answer key. I have learned that if I provided students with grids that they could glue on their cards, I unwittingly set in their minds the options for the x and y values. I find that when they create their own it works much better, so I have $\frac{1}{2}$- and $\frac{1}{4}$-inch graph paper available so they can cut out and paste their grids on the cards. Never tell the class how the game should work. Some teams deal cards and do a "fish" game, some turn cards up one at a time and call match when a triple shows up, others create a memory game. Student choice helps in providing insight into their understanding. You may also want to assign tasks to the students so that one does not become the "word problem" creator, and so on.

LESSON 2.2: LINEAR PROGRAMMING: IS THERE ALWAYS A SOLUTION?

Length: Four days

Unit Sequence	Teacher Reflections
Concepts C1, C7, C10, C11, C12, C13	
Principles P2, P3, P4, P5, P8, P9, P12, P13, P15, P16, P21	
Skills S1, S2, S3, S4, S5, S8, S9, S10, S11, S12, S13, S14	
Standards SD2, SD4, SD5, SD6, SD7, SD8, SD9, SD10, SD12, SD14, SD15	
Guiding Questions 1. Can we always find a common solution to a real-world problem? 2. What characteristics of our algebraic model enable us to determine whether a common solution can be found? 3. How can a mathematical model like a graph help us understand data? 4. Can a graph provide us with the exact answer to a real-world problem for every situation? 5. How does a graph help you determine the reasonableness of your answer? 6. How can the parts of an algebraic model give you clues about the graph? 7. When is it appropriate to use a fractional rate in a real-world model?	
Background Information	When you review the preceding lessons and combine that with student responses, you will come to realize that students may have the misconception that all linear programming scenarios will have a common solution in the first quadrant. They may also mistakenly believe that all systems will have "nice" whole-number answers. This is because students tend to generalize rather quickly, particularly since their experience with systems is limited. Students need to work with problems that do not have "tidy" whole-number answers. They need to work with systems that have rational solutions. Lesson 2.2 is designed to address that issue.

Unit Sequence	Teacher Reflections
Introduction	Introduce the lesson with some discussion about common solutions. Will walkers always meet up with one another? (What if they take different paths?) Will savers and spenders always have a point where they have equal amounts of money? Ask for examples.
Teaching Strategies and Learning Experiences *Day 1* **Resource 2.8: Will We Always Match?** is an opportunity to review common solutions and then look at situations that do not share a common solution. Students work in small groups. Problems 1, 2, and 3 are designed to have common solutions, while Problems 4 and 5 are designed to not have common solutions. Students may have difficulty with the first problem in deciding on the intervals. Let them puzzle with this dilemma. Problem 2 introduces a new notion with the baking time of 15 minutes per batch. Again, let students figure out a way to represent this on the grid and in their equation. Let them be creative. Check to see if students are using discrete points versus lines. Problem 3 should be easy for the students. It is crucial that Problem 3 be correct. Make sure that all students have the same equations. Again, students should be putting their answers on the transparency for all to see.	*Day 1* I suggest that you create overhead transparencies for these sheets so that student solutions can be presented. As a matter of classroom presentation practice, I take note of who has completed the transparency solution. That person cannot do the explaining: other people in the group need to explain, not surprisingly. Often the one who completes the answer sheet knows the most about the solution. That student needs to make sure that the group or team fully understands. Additionally, when working with linear functions, take care to interchange the variable term and constant. I have had many students in a formal algebra class make the following error: $y = 5 + 3x$, where they call 5 the slope and 3 the y-intercept, because they have been so accustomed to seeing the "slope" value in the first position and the intercept in the "second" position. Also, students need to be reminded that $y = 2x - 5$ is the same as $y = -5 + 2x$. This is always a big concern, especially when you go to graphing. Representing data is an important part of problem solving. If groups continue to struggle, you may want to provide them with a sheet of graph paper. Otherwise, hold back, ask questions, and do not provide the answers. Check to see that these data are continuous. Students will have a difficult time deciding on the intervals. Talk to them, but do not give them the answer. I am always surprised at the way students address the "dozen" component of this example. Walk around and see what your students do. They often are quite perplexed by the 15-minute piece. Most students are happy to work on Problem 3 because it is an easier task than the preceding questions. It is wise to mix problems of varying degrees of difficulty throughout. If your tack is to have all problems progressively more challenging, students can become discouraged and their endurance undermined.

Unit Sequence	Teacher Reflections
Problems 4 and 5 will not have points of intersection. The student explanations for these problems are important. Try to guide them to discussing the coefficient for the variable. Discussion about rates and slope should evolve.	Problems 4 and 5 present situations where there is no common point of intersection. I provided a situation for both positive and negative slope. Now is a good time to talk about consequences of a positive and a negative slope in a single situation and the likelihood of intersection. It is now a nice time to introduce solving equations with variables on both sides if the group is ready for that, or with students who are accelerated.
Closure **Resource 2.9: Drawing Conclusions** is a homework sheet for practice. The homework integrates numerous "families": same slopes, different intercepts, positive/negative slopes, same intercepts, and so on. It is intended that you engage the students in discussions of commonalities and differences. These are routine practice problems. Have the students start this in class to resolve any initial questions that may arise. Students will need graph paper for their work. They should still find five pairs of points to plot. Keep the graphing in Quadrant I, though you may wish to consider the entire coordinate plane when you go over their answers.	Another point worth mentioning *at the end* of the unit is the title. As adults, we know that this question opens the door for nonmatch options. Students are not skilled in noticing this subtle clue. We need to make them aware so that they have every advantage that we have. This worksheet is a good problem-solving sheet: the questions have components that are bigger than a single student, yet the foundation has been provided for them to be successful. Problem solving is messy and good problem solving requires some collaboration. We will further address the issue of slope and intersections in the next component. Note that two equations that have fractional coefficients are included. This is intentional and is intended to "just show up" on the homework. I hope that students will choose values that are multiples of the denominator. In doing so, the graphing can be accurate. For the earlier examples, the coefficient was an integer. Many students choose 0, 1, 2, 3, and 4. If they continue with this choice pattern, they may have trouble graphing the points. Discuss that when the coefficient is $\frac{1}{2}$, then values like 0, 2, 4, 6, and 8 are better choices, since the coordinate point comprises integers. Tomorrow's lesson can address this point. Since these problems are not restricted by a domain, the use of the entire coordinate plane can be woven into your discussion as appropriate. If your students have not had exposure to integers or rational numbers, you can stay in Quadrant I. There is a bonus question (Problem 7) that can be for those students who are clever.

Unit Sequence	Teacher Reflections
Day 2 and Maybe Day 3 It is important that you review all of the homework problems prior to today's lesson. If there are misconceptions, address them. It is also worth spending the time discussing slope, coefficients, y-intercepts, and so on to further develop connections between vocabulary, algebraic representations, graphs, and equations. For today's lesson, I wanted to separate the skill needed to manipulate the data versus the creation of the word problems. Additionally, you should introduce the negative fractional coefficient. Do not rush this lesson, hence the two-day recommendation made above. Spend time talking about similarities and differences. Be sure to use math vocabulary. Those slopes are coefficients for the variable, not "numbers in front of the letter." You may have students who have decided that, in restricting their information to Quadrant I, if the slopes are the same, the equations will not intersect and if the slopes are different, they will intersect. You can address that concern with Problem 7 from the homework. The preceding homework lesson provides the scaffold for today's lesson. A lesson that brings our favorite topic to the forefront is fractions. **Resource 2.10: Fractions, Graphs, and Solutions** addresses the topic of fractional rates. Students should be able to work through the problems in small groups or independently after some discussion about good choices for fractional coefficients. **Resource 2.11: Math Models and Real-World Solutions** integrates fractional rates with viable real-world solutions. Students should be able to comfortably move through these activities using algebraic models and graphs.	Correct use of vocabulary demystifies advanced math topics. Often it is vocabulary that intimidates novice mathematicians, when in fact correct vocabulary allows them to open the door to advanced math topics. *Day 2 and Maybe Day 3* Continue to have students generate five points for the graphs even though we know three points are adequate. By asking students to use five points, they get some extra practice. The class examples today are in that drill and practice mode with the homework utilizing the linear programming skills that have been developed. They have seen the negative slopes before, so just move along without a lot of fanfare. You will be surprised how they can "just do it" now. I know I was surprised when I first used this approach. My experience has led me to the belief that this novel approach enables students to acquire topics (integer/rational number manipulation) that are typically difficult at best when presented in the typical textbook computational units. It must be the avenue that we are using that makes is easier for the students. When students "prove their common solution," the nonalgebraic strategy would be to substitute the x-value into each equation to generate the y-value. If the solution is common, the same y-value will result in each. If your students are advanced, you can easily initiate the algebraic solving process with your students.

Unit Sequence	Teacher Reflections
	Again, my suggestion is to make a transparency and put the solutions on the overhead. Problems 3 and 4 are companions to the positive and negative slope using a fractional rate. I tend to try and just have the students logically puzzle this out. Even with limited integer experience, most if not all students can model the situation. As you walk around and monitor the groups, you will see where an intervention is needed, if one is needed at all.
Day 4	*Day 4*
Resource 2.12: Sometimes We Just Practice is included, and students will be practicing, just as the title suggests. Students should have developed some skills and strategies with graphing systems. There is one difference with the graphing systems presented in Resource 2.12. Included are some systems that do not have nice common points of intersections. The students are expecting all solutions to have integral values. In fact, we know that not all solutions will have integral values. Students need to understand this, as well. You can choose to approximate or continue to develop some equation solving. If you are going to approximate, $\frac{1}{2}$-inch graph paper is a fine solution. Some students may be clever enough to make partitions on the grid to reflect fractional pieces. In particular, Problem 3 presents a pair of perpendicular lines, Problem 4 is a system with parallel lines, and Problems 5 and 6 have fractional solutions.	**Resource 2.12: Sometimes We Just Practice** is a fairly straightforward drill exercise. You will be able to identify students who have the skills but are still struggling when they are required to create the linear equations or systems. If that is the case, you can have them create a problem to match the problems. There are some systems that intersect, but the intersection point does not have integral coordinate values. This is important to see, because we do not want the students to think that all the problems have "neat" answers. You may be surprised to see that students will "make" the point of intersection have integral values. Here is an opportunity for them to reconcile their graph with the example. They need to have confidence in their result, even though it may not be the result they had anticipated. You can generate lots of real-world examples where the common solution is not an integral point by asking the students to generate hypothetical situations.
Closure You may choose to use this activity as a formative assessment piece, if you have the time. It can add an entire period to the unit, however. If you are working in a block schedule, it can easily fit into Day 4. Use poster-sized grid paper to summarize student findings and then post them around the room. For each of the topics, groups will need to show the equation, a set of points, and a real-world problem to model the concepts. Have the students stay in Quadrant I. Each group should show samples of discrete and continuous examples, graphs that have a positive slope, graphs with a negative slope, fractional slopes, graphs that represent a family of parallel lines, and a system that has a solution, and a system that does not have a solution.	Again, it is always great to have students consolidate their learning. Additionally, this should enable you to note areas that still need attention. Try to focus on groups that really need your support rather than those that are working well, even though those are often the most exciting groups. Encourage students who are just beginning to master the topics to use their notes as models. Push students who are more adept with the skills to develop novel representations for each of the criteria.

LESSON 2.3: LINEAR PROGRAMMING AND REGRESSION: DATA AND SOLUTIONS CAN BE MESSY

Length: Two days

Unit Sequence	Teacher Reflections
Concepts C1, C2, C3, C4, C5, C7, C8, C12, C13, C14, C15, C16	
Principles P1, P2, P4, P5, P8, P13, P14, P18	
Skills S2, S3, S4, S5, S6, S7, S8, S9, S12, S14	
Standards SD2, SD3, SD4, SD5, SD6, SD7, SD8, SD9, SD10, SD12, SD13, SD14, SD15	
Guiding Questions 1. How is this activity different from the activities we have done earlier? 2. How can this model help us predict when it is not a perfect model? 3. Why is slope a more complicated problem in these activities when compared to the earlier activities? 4. Why are models important in mathematics? 5. How do models help us understand real-world relationships? 6. How are linear functions useful?	
Background Information	There comes a time when we need to introduce students to the messiness that can be the real world. This next lesson is that time. Nonetheless, the graph can enable students to predict answers to questions that are not as clear-cut as the perfect linear functions that we have seen throughout the unit. This activity can be used repeatedly with students when discussing the line of best fit and when using graphing calculators to find that line. If you choose to implement the calculator at this time, I would limit its use to the stat plot feature and "guessing" at the slope and the equation. To use linear regression without accompanying conceptual understanding undermines the goals for this unit.

Unit Sequence	Teacher Reflections
Introduction	I enjoy this activity, but with the healthy lifestyle requirements in schools, the M&Ms may not work. You could use those chewy fruit bites or those 16-bean soup mixes that use dried beans, though I would suggest focusing on only five to eight of the bean types in the mixtures or you will have too many to count. You may also want to give each child a cup with half of the contents of the bag. Then when you do class tallies, your running totals will be in $\frac{1}{2}$-bag increments. Don't forget paper plates so the candy or beans are not on desktops.
Teaching Strategies and Learning Experiences *Day 1* **Resource 2.13: The M&Ms Experiment** is an opportunity to demonstrate to the class that data are not always in a perfect linear relationship. Even when the data are not represented by a perfect linear model, however, the graph and relationship can provide a model that will enable you to make predictions. Gather data on a particular color of M&M (or bean, or fruit bite) and try to find lines that will represent the data. Use a running total data collection method here. Student 1: Bag 1, 10 reds—so the point is (1,10). Student 2: Bag 2, 8 reds—so the point is (2,8), and so on. The easiest way for the students to find a slope is to have them connect points with a straightedge. I find that they have trouble if they do not. You can have lots of discussion about lines of best fit and which would be the best one. **Resource 2.14: The M&Ms Experiment: Homework** is included as an optional homework sheet. You can use this sheet as appropriate for your classes. For this activity, you will need to gather class data. Pick a different color M&M and have the students complete the sheet at home.	*Day 1* I find it very interesting to look at how the students "organize" their piles of M&Ms; it is very telling, and may provide a glimpse into the learning style of your students. There is always that one student who will go online to find out if there is a certain distribution percentage. If so, it will lead to a fun discussion the next day. You can have highly motivated students find several "lines" that work and challenge them to find the "average" slope for that set of lines. In fact, this is what is known as "linear regression." It is an upper-level math concept, but certainly one that students can complete as it "makes sense" to them. It is easy to see that there are many slopes that work, yet there should be one that works the best. For other students who are at a more concrete level, finding two different slopes is adequate. It should be noted that *no matter the level*, *all* students can participate in the "finding the average slope" discussion. It is big-picture understanding, where we are using

Unit Sequence	Teacher Reflections
	linear functions to model real-world data. Finding data that are not "perfectly" related but that can be modeled using a linear relationship is the goal of this activity. You could do this average slope activity with an overhead grapher and use the stat plot feature. This way you could enter the student equations to see which of the equations best represents the data.
Day 2 **Resource 2.15: The Jumping Jacks Experiment** has students work with yet another type of data. It merits discussion on limits. What about resting heart rates and heart rates after exercise? Students can see that there are limits for these data. In fact, you would not "predict" values after a certain point. This is another important component in the representation of data and their meaningful real-world interpretation. Each data point is the student's resting pulse and her after-activity pulse. Some students will be challenged to figure out intervals for this activity: there are always a few outliers (students who have unusually low heart rates or unusually high heart rates). The effect of outliers can be discussed. In addition to this activity, have students think of situations where outliers have a great effect. For example, if 24 employees earn $30,000 per year each and the boss earns $1,000,000 per year, is an "average" salary for 25 people a good measure of average?	*Day 2* The data resulting from **Resource 2.15: The Jumping Jacks Experiment** make up one of those data sets that you might want to share with your physical education teachers. I have seldom been able to keep the class jumping for the entire two minutes. While I am wildly counting and cajoling them, I always have to stop when I notice that they are panting and their jumping jacks are more like a clap. So, use your best judgment for this activity. Additionally, students will have a difficult time taking their resting pulse, even going so far as to tell you that they do not have a pulse. It is worth noting that after jumping, they all exclaim that, "I can find it really easy now!"
Closure **Resource 2.16: Linear Programming Portfolio Task** is included as a potential formal final assessment. A scoring rubric is included. You may have students work in teams or individually. You can have students do their own problems on the large grid paper and post them around the room. The key here is to be flexible with your students and maximize their experience. You can administer the post-assessment **(Resource 2.17: Post-Assessment: What Do You Know About Word Problems and Functions?)** and compare the results with the pre-assessment **(Resource 2.1: Pre-Assessment: What Do You Know About Word Problems and Functions?)**. Share those results with the students.	We have now arrived at the close of the unit. I hope that you are pleasantly surprised at the level of mathematics that your students have been able to access. Students generally enjoy this activity because it is out of the norm for them. Remember, this sets the stage for higher-level math. As a facilitator of student learning, I hope you have enjoyed yourself as well.

SUGGESTED READINGS

Clement, J. (1989). The concept of variation and misconceptions in Cartesian graphing. *Focus on Learning Problems in Mathematics*, 11(1–2), 77–87.

Leinhardt, G., Zaslavsky, O., & Stein, M. (1990). Functions, graphs, and graphing: Tasks, learning, and teaching. *Review of Educational Research*, 60, 1–64.

National Council of Teachers of Mathematics (NCTM). (2000). *Principles and standards for school mathematics*. Reston, VA: Author.

Vergnaud, G., & Errecalde, P. (1980). Some steps in the understanding and the use of scales and axis by 10- to 13-year-old students. In R. Karplus (Ed.), *Proceedings of the fourth international conference for the psychology of mathematics education* (pp. 285–291). (ERIC Reproduction Service No. ED 250 186).

Wavering, M. (1985, April). *The logical reasoning necessary to make line graphs*. Paper presented at the annual meeting of the National Association for Research in Science Teaching, French Lick Springs, Indiana.

RESOURCES

The following Resources can be found at the companion website for *Parallel Curriculum Units for Mathematics, Grades 6–12* at www.corwin.com/math6–12.

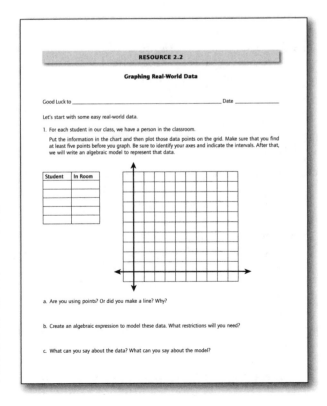

RESOURCE 2.3

Interesting Developments in Data

Good Luck to _____ Date _____

1. You are making chocolate chip cookies for class. You want each cookie to have five chips.

   Put the information in the chart and then plot those data points on the grid. Make sure that you find at least five points before you graph. Be sure to identify your axes and indicate the intervals. After that, we will write an algebraic model to represent that data.

a. Are you using points? Or did you make a line? Why?

b. Create an algebraic expression to model these data. What restrictions will you need?

c. What can you say about the data? What can you say about the model?

RESOURCE 2.4

Up and Down the Mountain: Will We Ever Meet?

Good Luck to _____ Date _____

1. Shontrell is a member of the school hiking club, "The Mountaineers." She has decided to hike up a nearby hill so she can build up her endurance. She hikes uphill at a nice brisk pace of four yards per minute.

   Put the information in the chart and then plot those data points on the grid. Make sure that you find at least five points before you graph. Be sure to identify your axes and indicate the intervals. After that, we will write an algebraic model to represent that data.

a. Are you using points? Or did you make a line? Why?

b. Create an algebraic expression to model these data. What restrictions will you need?

c. What can you say about the data? What can you say about the model?

RESOURCE 2.5

My Models and Graphs

Good Luck to _____ Date _____

For each of the problems, you will need to find five data points, graph those points in the first quadrant, and create a real-world problem that will model the data.

1. $y = 3x$

My word problem:

RESOURCE 2.6

The Match Game: Problems, Graphs, and Models

Good Luck to _____ Date _____

_____ _____

_____ _____

Your task is to create a matching game.

First, give your team a name, then list team member names below so I know who is on each team. The team name will be on a card and placed in the baggie with your game cards.

Before you begin, read through the scoring rubric to make sure that you meet all the criteria for assessment.

You will need to create eight sets of three for a total of 24 cards. Each set will have a word problem, the matching algebraic equation, and the correct graph to model that data. Three of the eight sets will need to be problems that have a common solution.

You will need to provide an answer key for your game.

You will play your game with your team to make sure everything is clear.

After your game is complete, you will hand in your baggie along with a card that has your game rules, the answer key, and your team name. Your team will then select one bag at a time and play the other teams' games. You will evaluate the games based on the Peer Assessment Scoring Rubric.

Make sure you put the team name on the peer evaluation form and your team name in the space for evaluator.

Have a good time, create interesting word problems, and make sure you have the correct answers.

RESOURCE 2.7

Peer Assessment Scoring Rubric

Scoring Team _____

Scored by Team _____

1. The game is complete with 24 game cards. (24 points)	_____
2. The graph cards have labeled axes and intervals and uniquely match the corresponding problem and equation. (8 points)	_____
3. The word problem cards are clearly written and uniquely match the corresponding graph and equation. (8 points)	_____
4. The algebra equations correctly match the word problem and uniquely match the corresponding graph. (8 points)	_____
5. Choose one score point. The problems in this game are mostly challenging (16 points) mostly average (8 points) mostly basic (4 points)	_____
Total Points Earned	_____

- -

Scoring Team _____

Scored by Team _____

1. The game is complete with 24 game cards. (24 points)	_____
2. The graph cards have labeled axes and intervals and uniquely match the corresponding problem and equation. (8 points)	_____
3. The word problem cards are clearly written and uniquely match the corresponding graph and equation. (8 points)	_____
4. The algebra equations correctly match the word problem and uniquely match the corresponding graph. (8 points)	_____
5. Choose one score point. The problems in this game are mostly challenging (16 points) mostly average (8 points) mostly basic (4 points)	_____
Total Points Earned	_____

RESOURCE 2.8

Will We Always Match?

Good Luck to _____ Date _____

1. You are finally going skiing this season. You get on the chairlift at the bottom of the mountain. It is moving slowly today since there are lots of people skiing. It is moving at the rate of two feet per second. You just texted Shaun, and it is 2:00 p.m. He is at the top of the mountain, about to start his run. You tell him you will wave as he skis under the lift. You know the mountain is 2,400 feet high and he is skiing down really fast at eight feet per second. How long will it be before you expect to see him skiing below the lift? How far down the mountain will he be? How much farther after you see him until you are at the mountaintop?

Your equation: _____ Shaun's equation: _____

I would expect to wave to Shaun at _____

Shaun would be _____ feet down the mountain.

I will have _____ feet to go until I am at the mountaintop.

RESOURCE 2.9

Drawing Conclusions

Good Luck to _____ Date _____

Use graph paper to complete these graphs. Be sure to include five sets of points and plot those points, and then graph the equation in Quadrant I. Be sure to label your axes and indicate the intervals you have used. In the case of a system, find the common solution if one exists. If there is no common solution, explain why.

Put the following three equations on a single grid. To make it easy to review your work, use a key. For example, you may use different colors for each problem.

1. $f(x) = 2x + 3$ 2. $s(t) = -2t + 3$ 3. $y = \frac{1}{2}x + 3$

Put the following three equations on a single grid. To make it easy to review your work, use a key. For example, you may use different colors for each problem.

4. $v(t) = -2t + 20$ 5. $y = 20 - 5x$ 6. $y = \frac{1}{4}x + 20$

Put each system of equations on a single grid. If there is a common solution in Quadrant I, find it. If there is not a common solution, explain why. Bonus: If you can find a common solution in a quadrant other than Quadrant I, find it. ☺

7. System 1   8. System 2   9. System 3

$$\begin{cases} y_1 = 3x + 4 \\ y_2 = 2x + 1 \end{cases} \quad \begin{cases} 6 - 2x = y_1 \\ 4 - 2x = y_2 \end{cases} \quad \begin{cases} y_1 = 10 - 2x \\ y_2 = 3x \end{cases}$$

RESOURCE 2.10

Fractions, Graphs, and Solutions

Good Luck to _____ Date _____

For all of the problems, you will need to find five data points and graph them in Quadrant I. Be sure to label your axes and indicate your intervals.

1. $y = \frac{1}{4}x + 1$

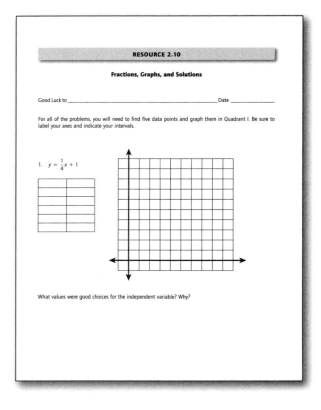

What values were good choices for the independent variable? Why?

RESOURCE 2.11

Math Models and Real-World Solutions

Good Luck to _____ Date _____

1. You have your first job because you need to save up enough money for a cell phone. You find a plan from Cheep Minutes that has you pay $20.00 per month plus $\frac{1}{4}$ cent or $0.025 per minute. You see another plan from UZE-This-Plan that has a $10.00 per month fee and charges $\frac{1}{2}$ or $0.005 cent per minute.

Create an algebraic model for each plan, find five points, and graph on the grid. Label axes and intervals; include a key.

Cheep Minutes: _____ UZE-This-Plan: _____

Will there ever be a time when you will pay the same amount? Explain.

RESOURCE 2.12

Sometimes We Just Practice

Good Luck to _____ Date _____

1. If possible, find a common solution for the following two equations. If not possible, explain why.

$\begin{cases} y_1 = 2x \\ y_2 = 10 - 2x \end{cases}$

Prove that this is a common solution:

2. If possible, find a common solution for the following two equations. If not possible, explain why.

$\begin{cases} y_1 = \frac{2}{3}x \\ y_2 = \frac{1}{2}x + 1 \end{cases}$

Prove that this is a common solution:

RESOURCE 2.13

The M&Ms Experiment

Good Luck to _____ Date _____

1. The total number of M&Ms in your bag: _____

Red: _____   Orange: _____   Green: _____   Yellow: _____   Brown: _____   Blue: _____

(Check the data and add all the colors; that number should equal the total number of M&Ms in the bag.)

2. Gather the data from the class:

	x Bag	y Total
1		
2		
3		
4		
5		
6		
7		
8		
9		
10		
11		
12		
13		
14		
15		
16		
17		
18		
19		
20		
21		

RESOURCE 2.14

The M&Ms Experiment: Homework

Good Luck to _____ Date _____

1. The total number of M&Ms in your bag: _____

Red: _____   Orange: _____   Green: _____   Yellow: _____   Brown: _____   Blue: _____

(Check the data and add all the colors; that number should equal the total number of M&Ms in the bag.)

2. Gather the data from the class:

	x Bag	y Total
1		
2		
3		
4		
5		
6		
7		
8		
9		
10		
11		
12		
13		
14		
15		
16		
17		
18		
19		
20		
21		

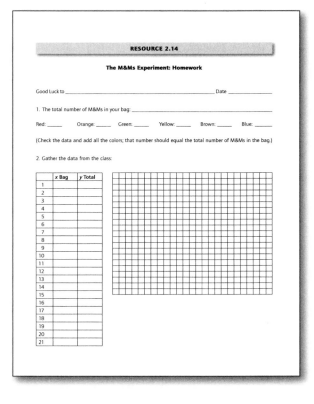

RESOURCE 2.15

The Jumping Jacks Experiment

Good Luck to _____ Date _____

1. Your resting pulse: count number of beats in 15 seconds and multiply by four to find beats per minute:
_____ beats in 15 sec. × 4 = _____ beats/minute

Your pulse after two minutes of jumping jacks: count number of beats in 15 seconds and multiply by four to find beats per minute: _____ beats in 15 sec. × 4 = _____ beats/minute

2. Gather the data from the class:

	x Rest	y Exercise	
1			
2			
3			
4			
5			
6			
7			
8			
9			
10			
11			
12			
13			
14			
15			
16			
17			
18			
19			
20			
21			

RESOURCE 2.16

Linear Programming Portfolio Task

Good Luck to _____ Date _____

You will be solving the following problem. You should read through the rubric to be sure that you have completed each task. You MUST graph on graph paper. Written explanations should be clear, and should use correct math vocabulary. Be sure to hand in the cover page with your task. I will return the cover page with your score. Good luck! ☺

You own two dogs. Gigantur is a very large dog so you buy him special healthy-weight food in 50-pound bags. He is on a special diet and can have $\frac{3}{2}$ pounds of dog food per day. You also have a small dog, Buttons. You buy her a special variety that comes in 30-pound bags. She gets $\frac{1}{4}$ of a pound per day.

1. Identify your variables.	(2 points)	Earned _____
2. Write an equation for Gigantur and Buttons (explain what the equation "says").	(8 points)	Earned _____
3. Make a table of values for each equation (you must have five pairs of points for each equation).	(10 points)	Earned _____
4. Graph both equations on the same quadrant.		
a. Label each axis.	(2 points)	Earned _____
b. Indicate the intervals on the axes.	(2 points)	Earned _____
c. Label the points.	(10 points)	Earned _____
d. Identify each graph (using colored pencils or a key).	(2 points)	Earned _____
5. Use your graph and predict when you will have the same amount in each bag.	(10 points)	Earned _____
6. Explain how you know this is correct.	(7 points)	Earned _____
7. After 12 days, how much will be left in each bag? Explain how you know.	(7 points)	Earned _____
8. How long will each bag of food last? Explain how you know.	(10 points)	Earned _____
9. Create your own linear equation problem where you have a common point of intersection; make it a real-world example.	(30 points)	Earned _____

RESOURCE 2.17

Post-Assessment: What Do You Know About Word Problems and Functions?

Good Luck to _____ Date _____

Write an algebraic equation using two variables to model the following situations. After you write an equation, create a graph to represent the situation. Use five values to create your graph.

1. How much will you earn if for each hour you work, you earn $1.00? _____
(2 points)

Table for Values (5 Points)   **Graph Your Values (5 points)**

Similarity

A Study in Relationships, Grade 10

Amy J. Germundson

INTRODUCTION TO THE UNIT

Geometric similarity is in essence "reasoning about proportions." Proportional thinking is a cornerstone of mathematics. It requires an in-depth understanding of number relationships in both a qualitative and quantitative sense. By the high school level, it is likely that students have been exposed to the foundational ideas of ratio, proportion, and scale. This unit revisits these notions in greater complexity and leads students toward an understanding of similarity through the conceptual lens of **relationships**.

What is a relationship? How can we define relationships mathematically? How can mathematical relationships be used to make sense of a situation, a context, or real-world problem? The idea of a **relationship** is a central concept on which the discipline of mathematics pivots. From representative topics such as fractions at the elementary level to trigonometric ratios at the high school level, students unravel this concept at different levels of complexity and across diverse contexts. Yet these topics often seem disconnected and unrelated to students when they are taught through an algorithmic and rules-oriented approach. This unit seeks a conceptual and explorative approach in which students are continuously challenged to connect the content and skills back to the organizing concept of relationships and larger principles and generalizations that are built on this concept. When teachers do so, students are challenged to see "beyond the numbers" and make sense of geometric similarity using the same type of transferable thinking processes and methodologies that experts engage in.

When designing this unit, the Parallels of Practice and Connections emerged to the forefront. Exemplifying the Curriculum of Practice, these lessons invite students to translate the organizing concept of relationships into mathematical applications, to select tools and appropriate resources to approach problems, to consider what type of evidence is needed to truly justify an idea or conjecture, to examine indicators of quality work in mathematics, and to engage in an intense focus on the inductive thinking processes that exemplify this discipline. The Curriculum of Connections logically extends from the Parallel of Practice through the realization that professionals and experts must be able to see the interconnectedness of knowledge to understand how the discipline functions in a larger scheme of knowledge. It is in these connections that students can see how mathematical concepts and approaches to thinking can be applied across differing contexts, how the notion of similarity in different fields and disciplines has been interpreted correspondingly and differently from how it is interpreted in the field of geometry, and how experts in fields such as architecture and literature use proportional reasoning as a form of communication in their own work. Questions throughout the unit are written to prompt and highlight thinking related to the Curriculum of Practice and the Curriculum of Connections.

The unit contains four foundational and model lessons that connect the ideas of ratio, proportion, and proportional reasoning to geometric similarity and the applications of similarity. It should be noted that this unit is not exhaustive of all content and can be expanded under the umbrella of the primary unit principles and generalizations to include topics such as perimeter, area of similar polygons, and proportional segments.

In the interest of instructional time, the learning experiences in this unit were purposefully chosen to maximize access to mastering the unit principles and generalizations and skills that derive from the national standards. However, there are many additional explorations and related topics that enrich this unit. To eliminate ragged time when a large number of students need help or when students finish with a task or assessment early, establish an anchor station, anchor activities (Tomlinson, 2003), or an area in your classroom where students can work independently. For this particular unit, investigations or readings related to the golden ratio, cartography, architecture, or constructing dilations would be an excellent extension of learning.

CONTENT FRAMEWORK

Organizing Concepts

Discipline-Specific Concepts

Ratio, Proportion, Similarity, Communication

Macroconcept

Relationships

Principles and Generalizations

Overarching Principle

P1: Relationships between numbers and shapes can be used both qualitatively and quantitatively to communicate ideas and help us make sense of a situation or real-world problem.

Supporting Principles

P2: Proportional reasoning can be utilized in a wide variety of contexts and settings to solve and make sense of real-world situations.

P3: Ratios function as a mathematical tool to reveal significant relationships.

P4: Proportions involve multiplicative relationships.

P5: Geometric similarity functions as a powerful analytic tool in the discipline of mathematics.

P6: Geometric similarity is the means of communicating ideas through time and culture, and in different contexts.

P7: Geometric patterns can be used to make generalizations about mathematical relationships.

National Mathematics Standards

SD1: Numbers and Operations

1.1: Understand relationships among numbers

SD2: Algebra

2.1: Use mathematical models to represent and understand quantitative relationships

2.4: Analyze change in various contexts

SD3: Geometry

3.1: Analyze characteristics and properties of two- and three-dimensional geometric shapes and develop mathematical arguments about geometric relationships

3.4: Use geometric modeling to solve problems in and gain insights into other disciplines and other areas of interest such as art and architecture

SD6: Problem Solving

6.1: Build new mathematical knowledge through problem solving; solve problems that arise in mathematics and in other contexts; apply and adapt a variety of appropriate strategies to solve problems; monitor and reflect on the process of mathematical problem solving

SD7: Reasoning and Proof

7.1: Make and investigate mathematical conjectures, selecting and using various types of reasoning and methods of proofs

SD8: Communication

8.1: Clearly communicate mathematical thinking, using the language of mathematics to precisely express mathematical ideas

SD9: Connections

9.1: Recognize and use connections among mathematical ideas; understand how mathematics ideas interconnect and build on one another; recognize and apply mathematics in contexts outside mathematics

Skills

S1: Identify ratios in a real-world data set

S2: Justify the importance of ratios as a mathematical tool

S3: Apply proportional reasoning to a variety of contexts and settings

S4: Connect the concepts of ratio, proportion, and relationship

S5: Utilize mathematical patterns to derive a definition of geometric similarity

S6: Compare and contrast the concept of similarity across fields and disciplines

S7: Explain geometric similarity as a means of communication

S8: Apply geometric similarity to communicating an idea or perspective

S9: Identify similarity "shortcuts"

S10: Justify why similarity shortcuts are creditable

S11: Apply the principles of triangle similarity to solve real-world problems via indirect measurement

ASSESSMENTS

Pre- and Post-Assessments

This set of four lessons on relationships includes a matched pre- and post-assessment. The matched assessments at the beginning and end of the unit challenge students to solve ratio and proportion tasks across contexts and make conceptual links between these concepts and the larger world of mathematics.

Formative Assessments

Five formal, formative assessments activities are included in this unit. These include a concept map activity, a practice sheet (Lesson 3.1), a thinking prompt, a differentiated investigation (Lesson 3.2), and a performance task (Lesson 3.3). The concept map is designed to reveal a student's emerging understanding of relationships, across disciplines; the practice sheet seeks to uncover a student's understanding of ratio and proportion. The two formative assessments in Lesson 3.2 probe students' understanding of the concept of similarity in geometry. The performance task in Lesson 3.3 requires students to apply their learning about the unit concepts (i.e., relationships, ratio, scale similarity) to a new situation—a proposal for a museum exhibit featuring the Giza Pyramids. The investigation in Lesson 3.4 will provide the teacher with information about students' understanding of the principles of similarity as they relate to triangles.

UNIT SEQUENCE, DESCRIPTION, AND TEACHER REFLECTIONS

LESSON 3.1: EXPLORING MATHEMATICAL RELATIONSHIPS

Length: Two days

Unit Sequence	Teacher Reflections
Concepts Ratio, Proportion, Relationship	
Principles and Skills P1, P2, P3, P4, S1, S2, S3, S4	
Standards SD1.1, SD2.1, SD2.4, SD3.1, SD3.4, SD6.1, SD9.1	
Introduction Begin the unit with a web brainstorm focused on the concept of relationships (see **Resource 3.1: Think About It: What Is a Relationship?**). What characterizes a relationship? What isn't a relationship? Why are relationships important? 　Allow students to brainstorm individually and then in pairs or small groups. Monitor groups to assess prior knowledge and possible misconceptions. End with a whole-class discussion and synthesis of ideas that give insight into this concept. Point out to students that they will be looking at relationships in the context of mathematics in the coming days. What is the nature of mathematical relationships? How does a mathematician establish and define relationships? How do mathematical relationships help us make sense of the world?	An organizing concept of this unit is relationships. Specifically, students will explore mathematical relationships between numbers and shapes that ultimately give rise to ideas such as ratio, proportion, and similarity. Most students will have some notion of what a "relationship" means from other disciplines and from their own lives. A web brainstorm serves the purposes of (1) activating prior knowledge, (2) assessing student knowledge and possible misconceptions, and (3) developing a common set of attributes that characterize this concept. In this unit, students will further build their understanding of relationships in the context of mathematics. *Teacher Note.* Save these web brainstorms. After Lesson 3.4, students will be prompted to synthesize their understandings of mathematical relationships and reflect on the progress they have made in their thinking.
Teaching Strategies and Learning Experiences See **Resource 3.2: Pre-Assessment**. Have students complete this brief pre-assessment that includes the essential knowledge, skills, and principles of the unit, as well as basic mathematical skills you anticipate students should have coming into this unit (see **Resource 3.3: Pre-Assessment Key**).	Two to three weeks before beginning this set of four lessons, administer the pre-assessment to students that is included at the end of this lesson. Make sure to emphasize that they will not be graded on the pre-assessment. Explain that the purpose of the data from the pre-assessment is to help you figure out where and how you will begin your instruction on the macroconcept, relationships.

Unit Sequence	Teacher Reflections
	Teacher Note. By high school, students might have a wide range of entry points into the unit learning objectives. A pre-assessment provides a quick glimpse at where students are in relation to the essential content. This pre-assessment highlights student thinking with regard to recognizing proportional relationships—specifically reasoning with a multiplicative versus an additive approach. Students who are advanced on this pre-assessment will be able to (1) solve ratio and proportion tasks across contexts and (2) make conceptual connections between these concepts into the bigger picture of mathematical relationships. On-grade-level learners will be able to provide a general approach to solving ratio and proportion tasks. They may lack larger connections, but the foundational skills for making these connections are present. Below-grade-level learners are not able to recognize a ratio or proportion. These students often seek a set of rules or algorithms without engaging in the critical thinking behind these tasks. It is imperative that these students work toward the unit generalizations and principles (getting to the big ideas or conceptual framework—the "so what?") while receiving scaffolding in the skills areas where they are weak.
Part I *Teacher Note.* Students who are advanced on the pre-assessment should proceed to the task listed under Ascending Intellectual Demand. **Interactive Mini-Lesson: What Is a Ratio? (Whole Class, Pair-Share)** • Ratio (relationship between two or more quantities) *Probing Question.* Why is a ratio defined as a relationship? • Examples of ratios across settings *Probing Question.* How does a ratio operate as its own entity (different from the individual quantities compared)? • Ratio notation and mathematical communication (words, odds, fractional) Highlight the importance of a mathematical vocabulary in communicating ideas. **Investigating Ratios as a Mathematical Tool** *Guiding Question.* How do ratios function as a mathematical tool to reveal significant relationships "hidden" in a data set?	*Part I* It is important that students have a solid grasp on the concept of a ratio when developing proportional reasoning. Realizing that the term "ratio" has most likely been introduced at an earlier grade, revisiting this idea through the conceptual lens of **relationships** strengthens and extends student understanding. Examples of ratios should focus on part-to-whole relationships (for example, ratio of the number of boys in the class to the total number of students in the class), part-to-part relationships (for example, ratio of the number of boys in the class to the number of girls in the class), and rates (for example, speed—numbers with differing units, feet per second, yards per second). Using examples across settings allows students to transfer their thinking to diverse contexts. Also highlighted in this part of the lesson is mathematical communication. Experts in the discipline know how to express numerical relationships accurately. Thus, the correct use of ratio notation and language is important in conveying ideas.

Unit Sequence	Teacher Reflections
Investigation by Interest Groups Explain to students that mathematical thinking often involves finding relationships via ratios in a set of data. Give students the choice of analyzing one real-world data set from diverse disciplines and fields (population studies, finance, sports, and so on). Working in small groups prompts students to find potential ratios. Follow-up questions include these: 1. What quantities did you relate and why? 2. What notation(s) could you use to communicate your ratio? What makes the most sense? Why? 3. What is the practical significance of your ratios in the setting you are studying? How would you use these ratios to assess the current situation and why? 4. In what other settings could you use ratios as a tool for revealing significant relationships? Combine two groups and have students share findings for Questions 1–4. **Whole-Class Discussion** • How can ratios be a helpful mathematical tool? • What type of mathematical thinking did you need to do in this investigation? What was challenging? • How can this type of mathematical thinking be applied in a variety of fields and disciplines?	A hallmark of mathematical thinking is the ability to find relationships among data and make sense of these relationships in a practical way. Ratios are one tool that can be used to reveal significant relationships. In this investigation, students employ mathematical thinking as they are challenged to (1) identify potential ratios in real-world sets of data, (2) mathematically communicate these ratios in a logical fashion, and (3) critically think about the use of these ratios. For example, business professionals often use the current ratio (current assets/current liabilities) to assess the financial strength of a firm and its ability to pay off debts in the coming year. Interest is a great motivator in the classroom. In this investigation, allow students to work in small collaborative groups with data sets they find meaningful. The authentic resources for this portion of the unit are easy to locate. Data sets for public use are available for download from the Internet. For example, • the Data and Story Library contains online data sets specifically for use by educators: http://lib.stat.cmu.edu/DASL; and • the American Statistical Association contains an educators' section with helpful resources: http://www.amstat.org/education/index.cfm
Ascending Intellectual Demand task (in lieu of the mini-lesson and investigation) Students ultimately determine and justify an answer to the following question: 　　Can ratios be used as a predictive tool? 　　Given a longitudinal data set, students are to choose one to two ratios (either on their own or with the help of an "expert" description that you provide for more-challenging ratios) and determine a method of systematically analyzing the ratios over time. In a letter to the CEO or other leader, students provide an analysis of the company or situation, a prediction for the future, and a discussion of how valid ratios are as a predictive tool.	In this task, advanced students explore the utility of ratios as a mathematical tool (same learning objective as the remainder of the class), but at a higher level of complexity and depth.

Unit Sequence	Teacher Reflections
Ratio Enrichment Challenge all students to find ratios in magazines, newspapers, or journals and post them on a designated wall in the classroom. These ratios can be used to prompt discussions throughout this unit.	
Part II **Comparing Equivalent Ratios: Proportional Reasoning** 1. Pose the following situation and allow pairs of students to grapple with it: Rob—a beginning photographer—would like to enlarge a photograph of his new car on his computer. He stretches the height by a couple of centimeters or so and then extends the width. He tries to do this several times but his car looks distorted. He asks you for some advice. Thinking about the idea of ratios, what feedback could you give him? Draw a picture. Give students time to think, and then engage them in a whole-group discussion of this situation. Through questioning, guide students toward the concept of proportion. For an image to be proportional after enlargement, what must be true about the relationship between the height and width ratios of the images? 2. Pose a formal definition and symbolic notation of proportion, emphasizing that it is an equivalent and multiplicative relationship between ratios. Briefly review how to set up and solve proportion problems. *Probing Question.* How could you define proportion in the light of "relationships"? 3. Proportion Stations: Set up four stations around the room and allow students to proceed individually or with a partner through these stations at their own pace. *Teacher Note.* You may need three or four of these stations. *Station 1:* Anna can bike 20 miles in 30 minutes. Sarah can bike 9 miles in 15 minutes. Who is the faster biker? Please show two ways you could solve this problem. Which way is easier for you to understand and why?	*Part II* This situation builds on the idea of a ratio and guides students toward a conceptual understanding of proportion. Monitor group discussion for possible misconceptions and address these as a whole class. Encourage students to begin thinking of proportion as a relationship between *two* relationships. Each station engages students in different aspects of proportional reasoning. Since students are at different readiness levels in relation to proportional reasoning, this is a great opportunity to walk around and provide scaffolding for students who are struggling. Additionally, post challenge questions at some of the stations for students who are ready to extend their thinking. Part of this station prompts metacognitive thinking. It is important for students to understand their own ways of thinking in this discipline.

Unit Sequence	Teacher Reflections
Station 2: Algebraic Connection. What does **proportion** look like graphically? A line is defined by the following equation: $$y = 3x$$ • Make a chart that reflects at least five points on this line. When you increase x, what happens to y? • Make a graph of this equation. Select three to four points on this line and compare the y/x ratios. How is the idea of direct proportion related to slope in the equation $y = 3x$? What does **proportion** look like graphically? *Challenge.* Write a real-life situation that tells the story of this equation.	In Station 2, students look at the idea of proportion in a graphical sense (another way of approaching mathematical thinking). The prompt guides students toward an algebraic representation of direct proportion—a special case of linear relationships. This station also serves to show students that the idea of proportion bridges fields of mathematics. The prompting questions guide students toward reaching the conclusion that y and x are proportional variables.
Station 3: To estimate wildlife populations, scientists often use a catch, tag, and release method. Suppose 16 elk were captured, tagged, and released back into their habitat. Two months later, 16 elk were captured. Of these elk, four were tagged (that is, had been caught, tagged, and released before). From this information, scientists could estimate the elk population. How many estimated elk are in the area? Describe your reasoning. With what other types of situations or careers could you use this type of proportional reasoning? *Challenge.* How accurate is this estimation? What variables could influence this?	One goal of Station 3 is to expose students to this type of mathematical thinking in other career fields.
Station 4: Stacy asks you if she can use a copy machine to reduce an 8" × 10" photograph to a 4" × 6" size. Is this possible? Why or why not?	
4. Wrap up this segment of the lesson with whole-class discussion focused on the bigger ideas of the stations (how to think about proportion mathematically, differing ways to represent proportion, connecting this concept across fields of mathematics, and so on).	Purposeful mathematics curriculum connects students to the world they live in. This last learning experience provides students an opportunity to explore how ideas of proportion are meaningful in the field of science and in daily life.
5. Review and extend with the following connection: Mathematical proportion is central to understanding topics and key laws in physics, chemistry, and other fields of science.	

Unit Sequence	Teacher Reflections
General Form of Direct Proportion: $y = mx$ In the equation $y = mx$, we see that $Y \propto x$. The quantities x and y increase in the same proportion. The slope (m) is a constant of proportionality. *Question (Individual or Pairs).* Newton's second law of motion states that force is equivalent to an object's mass times its acceleration, or $F = ma$. • What two variables are directly proportional in this equation? • Assuming the mass of the object is constant, if you quadruple the force on the object (such as when you hit a softball), what happens to the acceleration of the object? How do you know? Does this make sense scientifically? Present students with the following article from *e! Science News* and challenge them to describe how scientists used proportional reasoning to arrive at a scientific conclusion.	This article can be downloaded from http://esciencenews.com. In the search bar, enter the article title: "Stretchy Spider Silks Can Be Springs or Rubber."

Closure
 	
Have students complete **Resource 3.4: What Do You Know? Ratios and Proportions** individually.
 	
Exit Slip or Ticket Out of the Lesson
 	
What is the nature of proportional relationships? Or, how would you describe proportional relationships? Why are they helpful to us in making sense of situations?
  Give one example of a proportional relationship.
	This practice sheet provides a more formal piece of formative assessment. Students are given the opportunity to engage in a self-assessment, return to the primary concepts of this lesson and make connections, and apply their learning to various problem-solving situations. After providing feedback to each student, this practice sheet should alert the teacher if any reteaching is needed in future lessons.
	  This question probes students' thinking regarding a big idea of this lesson. It is important for students to grasp the idea that proportional relationships are multiplicative in nature (versus additive—a common misconception). The exit slips can quickly paint a picture of student understanding.

Unit Sequence	Teacher Reflections
	Scaffolding
	If students are struggling with the idea of additive versus multiplicative relationships, provide the following task individually or in small groups. This task has multiple arguments, additive and multiplicative in nature. Discuss this task in small groups and as a whole class to gain insight into students' thinking. Use questioning to help them see the difference between additive and multiplicative approaches. Knowing this difference is a key skill in being a proportional thinker.
	Task
	Julie is charting plant growth over time and has the following data:

Type of plant	Initial height (cm)	Height (cm) after five weeks
Strawberry	5 cm	10 cm
Sunflower	15 cm	20 cm

Question: After five weeks, which plant grew the most? Develop at least two mathematical arguments.

Teacher Note. For students needing additional challenge, add in a data point at five weeks. This increases the complexity of the analysis.

LESSON 3.2: IN SEARCH OF SIMILARITY

Length: One to two days

Unit Sequence	Teacher Reflections
Concepts Similarity, Proportion, Patterns, Relationships	
Principles and Skills P2, P7, S3, S5, S6	
Standards SD1.1, SD3.1, SD3.4, SD6.1, SD9.1	
Introduction Even authors use the concept of proportion. To review proportional reasoning from the previous lesson and to connect the concept of proportion to its use in literature, refer to Shel Silverstein's *One Inch Tall* (Silverstein, 1974). Read the poem as a class and have students, individually or in pairs, analyze this poem through a mathematical lens. • How does Silverstein make use of proportional reasoning in this poem? • Are the proportions accurate? Justify your thinking mathematically. Finish with a lively class discussion. Convey to students that in Lesson 3.2: In Search of Similarity they will apply the foundational concept of proportion (equivalent relationship between ratios) to developing another mathematical idea— similarity.	This prompt is meant to help students see that proportional reasoning can be used in many different contexts—even in literature.
Teaching Strategies and Learning Experiences *Introducing Similarity* Ask students if they have heard the term "similarity" before. Explain that experts across the disciplines have defined this term slightly differently. Have students examine the definition of this term in different fields and disciplines (see **Resource 3.5: Thinking Prompt**) and	The opening learning experience challenges students to consider the concept of similarity across disciplines and fields. Students should conclude that all definitions of similarity imply a relationship reflecting likeness between two or more ideas, texts, and so on. However, the degree of this likeness is difficult to interpret. Why?

Unit Sequence	Teacher Reflections

identify commonalities among the definitions. Convey to students that they have the opportunity to explore how the field of geometry defines this concept. How does this definition compare or contrast with other disciplines and fields?
 	
In Search of Similarity:
Concept Attainment Model
 	
Guiding Questions. How can geometric patterns be used to make generalizations about geometric relationships? What defines the relationship between similar figures?
 	
   Explain to students the importance of finding patterns in mathematical thinking. Present students with **Resource 3.6: Investigation: In Search of Similarity,** adding more examples and nonexamples of similar figures as necessary to work through individually or with a partner. This investigation challenges students to derive the relationship between similar figures by finding patterns in examples and nonexamples of the concept. The follow-up questions probe thinking related to the guiding questions.
 	
Ascending Intellectual Demand
 	
The last question of this investigation challenges students to extend their learning into designing a methodology that confirms or denies the following statement:
   All circles are similar.
	Yet another hallmark of mathematical thinking is finding patterns in data to uncover generalizations and make sense of situations. A concept attainment model allows students to arrive at a concept via this type of inductive logic.
	   Monitor student work and discussions for understanding. Scaffold and extend where needed.
	
	   Not all students are expected to complete this last question. However, students who are ready to extend their thinking have the opportunity to do so. Students should utilize proportional reasoning to determine if all circles are indeed the same shape. Students should arrive at the conclusion that all circles are similar (ratio of the circumference to the diameter is a constant).

Closure Using a student-led discussion, write the geometric definition of similarity on the board. Introduce the mathematical symbol for similarity and the ratio of similitude. Ask students to identify the ratios of similitude in the investigation.	Focus on the importance of a mathematical vocabulary in communicating ideas.

Unit Sequence	Teacher Reflections

Review the following questions:
 	
• How did you arrive at the definition of similarity? What was appealing about this type of thinking? What was frustrating?
• How is the interpretation of similarity in geometry the same as other disciplines and fields? How is it different? Why might this be?
 	
Collect the investigation and provide formative feedback. Assign students 5 to 10 similarity problems for additional practice.
 	
Exit Slip or Ticket Out of the Lesson
 	
1. Draw a figure labeled $\triangle DEF$ that is similar to $\triangle ABC$.
 	
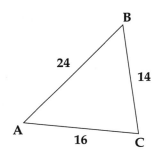
 	
2. How is similarity a function of mathematical relationships?
	This question challenges students to think about similarity in multiple disciplines. How is geometric similarity consistent with other interpretations? How is mathematical similarity unique in its interpretation?
	    Practice problems can be found in traditional mathematics textbooks. It is important to choose a representative and meaningful set of problems to process with students.
	    This exit slip serves as a quick piece of formative assessment. A glance over these cards provides a sense and measure of student understanding and growth as indicated by (1) the ability to apply similarity conditions to solving a problem and (2) the ability to "see" the nature of mathematical relationships within the concept of similarity.

LESSON 3.3: SIMILARITY AS A MEANS OF COMMUNICATION

Length: One to two days

Unit Sequence	Teacher Reflections
Concepts Relationships, Similarity, Communication	
Principles and Skills P1, P6, S7, S8	
Standards SD1.1, SD3.1, SD3.4, SD6.1, SD8.1, SD9.1	
Introduction *Teammates Consult* Experts often review their work with peers for feedback. Place students in small groups to review the practice problems from the prior day. Monitor groups for significant problems or issues. Briefly review major stumbling blocks as a class. *Modification for Learner Need* Based on the exit slip from the previous lesson, this would be a great time to work intensively with individual learners or small groups of learners that are struggling with the curriculum goals.	It is important to recognize that students are in a learning cycle and should not be penalized by a low grade during this time. In this situation, the students have time to process with scaffolding and support as needed. Feedback is immediate. *Teacher Note.* Students who finish quickly may work at one of the anchor stations.
Teaching Strategies and Learning Experiences *Teacher Note.* Prior to the students' arrival, hang three to five pictures of ancient maps, geoglyphs, and scale drawings or visuals that reflect history and culture around the classroom. *Similarity and Communication* *Probing Question.* Is math a form of communication? Why or why not? 1. Pose this question to the students and let them discuss. Explain to students that in this lesson they will investigate this question in multiple ways. In small groups, have students rotate around the room and synthesize an answer to the following questions:	The visuals may be obtained with help from your media specialist or a humanities colleague; you might also find them online. The famous cave paintings of Lascaux are a great example of scale drawings.

Unit Sequence	Teacher Reflections
• How do these visuals "tell a story" of history? • How have cultures been able to preserve history through these visuals? Guide students toward the understanding that people have utilized geometric similarity (or reasoning about proportion) as a means of depicting a way of life, the geography of a region, and so on. 2. Review the notion of scale and scale factor through an interactive minilesson (focusing on the connection to ratio). Provide an example of an architectural scale drawing to show students what "expert" work looks like and the indicators of quality it entails. 3. Present students with the performance task titled **Resource 3.7: Performance Task: On the Grand Scale.** Tell students that they will be using their understanding of number relationships via ratio, proportion, and similarity to "paint a perspective." Students may work individually or in pairs. This task may be done in one chunk of time or over the coming days in short periods (or during ragged time). *Teacher Note.* Conduct 5- to 10-minute minisessions on the process of design, writing abstracts, and constructing scale drawings. These can be implemented as needed. *Ascending Intellectual Demand* Students needing depth and complexity should have the option of developing a quantitative or qualitative protocol to assess the museum proposals. "Looking at expert work, what are indicators of a quality abstract or scale drawing?" "How can these be measured?" "How does your own work measure up to this protocol?" "What are some steps you can take to improve and grow?"	Students should observe pieces of work such as blueprints and scale drawings created by professionals in differing fields and disciplines. This not only offers them a standard of quality after which to pattern their own work, but also shows them the types of products experts work on. The goals of this performance task are (1) to assess student understanding of ratio, proportion, and similarity in an applied setting; (2) to give students the opportunity to explore geometric similarity in a different context; and (3) to engage students in work of product design. Through this authentic task, students develop a mathematical proposal including an abstract, scale drawing, and a reflective piece of writing. Working toward an authentic product allows student to see the "So what?" of mathematics. The performance task as written is rigorous and allows students some freedom in expression. Be prepared to scaffold as needed for struggling students. It may be helpful for them to be provided additional guiding questions that facilitate the design process. This task increases the degree of challenge by prompting students to think about defensible criteria against which they can assess their own work.

Unit Sequence	Teacher Reflections
Closure At the end of this task, have students share the scale drawings. *Probing Question.* Looking at all of the drawings, how can the notion of geometric similarity function as a means of communication? What drawings make the most impact and why— mathematically? Individually have students respond to one of the following prompts: • Thinking about what you have learned so far in this unit (ratio, proportion, similarity), construct a visual that shows the importance of understanding number relationships in making sense of the world. • A middle school student asks you why it is important to study number relationships. Why does it matter in the real world? So what? In light of what you have learned this far via ratio, proportion, and similarity, what response would you give to this student?	This prompt is a formative assessment. The situation challenges students to synthesize the knowledge and skills of the past lessons into addressing the overarching idea of this unit. At this point in the unit, students should be able to demonstrate progress toward developing larger conceptual understandings of geometric similarity and number relationships. Both prompts converge toward a common learning objective. However, students may choose to respond in a way the fits their learning modality or to respond in terms of their interest.

LESSON 3.4: INVESTIGATING TRIANGLE SIMILARITY

Length: One to two days

Unit Sequence	Teacher Reflections
Concepts Relationships, Similarity	
Principles and Skills P1, P5, S9, S10, S11	
Standards SD1.1, SD3.1, SD3.4, SD6.1, SD7.1, SD9.1	
Introduction Begin class with the following questions: • Triangle Congruency vs. Similarity: What can you say at this point? • How does the discipline of mathematics seek knowledge? How is this different from how other disciplines seek knowledge? After discussion, explain to students that they will be using mathematical thinking to determine if there are similarity "shortcuts" with triangles.	The purpose of the first question is to activate prior knowledge (specifically conditions or "shortcuts" related to triangle congruence) and address any misconceptions between the ideas of congruency and similarity. The second question challenges students to think about the discipline as a whole. Beyond what a math textbook states, how would an expert figure out if there are similarity conditions? What types of thinking and "testing" are involved?

Teaching Strategies and Learning Experiences
 	
1. Propose the following task to students: Your mission today is to determine and *justify* the existence or nonexistence of similarity shortcuts (as we saw with triangles). The shortcuts under question are AAA (angle-angle-angle), SSS (side-side-side), SAS (side-angle-side), and SSA (side-side-angle). Refer to **Resource 3.8: Investigation: Justify It! Triangle Similarity** at the end of this unit.
 	
Tools for Use: protractor, graph paper, tracing paper, compass, ruler, and your brain.
 	
2. Model this type of thinking as a whole class using AAA. Provide model questions to help students learn how to go about this type of thinking: What are the two essential pieces of information we need to determine if any two polygons are similar? Is AAA a similarity shortcut? Where do we begin our thinking (specifically, what are the tools available to us)? and so on. Let students work together while you check in with the class as a whole.
	An important goal of mathematics curriculum and instruction is process development. What transferable skills do we want students to leave our units with in addition to the "content"? This task engages students in thinking skills central to the discipline of mathematics (and arguably other fields and disciplines): analysis, synthesis, seeking patterns, and justifying. Thus, students use the idea of triangle similarity as a vehicle for developing key process skills in the discipline. How do experts think?
	  When students use key process skills, they arrive at the "why" behind the facts, conjectures, and theorems that otherwise are easily memorized and then forgotten over time.
	  Having "help or prompting" cards, in addition to teacher scaffolding, is a good way to support struggling learners.

Unit Sequence	Teacher Reflections
For the remainder of the exploration, allow students to work at their own pace. Anticipate that some students will be able to work very independently on this while others may need scaffolding. *Modification for Learner Need* For struggling learners, have "help" cards available for each similarity shortcut. These cards should not dictate the solution but can provide aids to facilitate their thinking. For example, for SSS, help cards might be as follows: Let's draw two triangles in which the sides are proportional, and let's label the triangles ABC and DEF. If you know that the sides are proportional (one similarity condition), what can you say about the angles? Why? How do you know? 3. Provide practice problems for students that allow them to apply these shortcuts. Highlight the purpose of using shortcuts. *Probing Question.* How can knowing these types of relationships serve as an analytic tool for making sense of situations and real-world problems? *Exploration.* Indirect Measurement with Similar Triangles. Explain to students that triangle similarity shortcuts and relationships function as a powerful analytic tool in making sense of real-world situations that involve indirect roads or paths to a destination. Illustrate this to students by engaging them in the following task: A scientist asks you for help determining the height of an unusual species of very tall cactus. Clearly, traditional methods of measurement are not going to work in this situation (ouch). However, you have a quick and reliable method for determining the height. On a sunny day, you determine that the six-foot scientist casts a shadow of four feet. At the same time during the day, the cactus casts a shadow of nine feet. Using this information, find a way to determine the height of the cactus. Challenge students to consider how their knowledge of number relationships helped them to arrive at a conclusion.	

Unit Sequence	Teacher Reflections
Allow students to use their knowledge, skills, and understandings of geometric similarity to solve this problem. Follow up with other real-world situations. *Ascending Intellectual Demand* For students who have a clear understanding of these concepts (determined by their thinking and performance in the cactus problem and thus far in the unit) *and* are ready for a task higher on the expertise spectrum, pose the following question in lieu of the follow-up problems (pairs of students would be ideal for this): Using only a mirror, a meter stick, and yourself, determine the height of this classroom indirectly. *Hint.* Turn to physics. Find out how light hits a mirror. Explain your procedure and conclusions. Measure the height of the classroom directly. How close are the indirect and direct measurements? What are some possible sources of error?	This task challenges students to connect what they understand about triangle similarity and indirect measurement in an unusual and unfamiliar setting. Have a physics textbook on hand as a resource in this unit. The key to solving this problem is understanding that when light hits a mirror, the angle of incidence is equivalent to the angle of reflection. Furthermore, if a student puts a mirror on the ground and steps back until she can see the top of a wall, the following distances can be recorded: 1. Height of student (to eyes) 2. Distance from the middle of the mirror to the student 3. Distance from the middle of the mirror to wall Combining these data, students will be able to establish similar triangles and solve for the unknown variable of height.
Closure *Exit Slip* How do mathematics professionals translate the fundamental concept of number relationships into practice? Provide an example or piece of evidence that supports your answer. (Think about what you have learned so far.)	This question prompts students to interpret the anchoring concepts and ideas of the discipline into practice.

CONTINUATION OF UNIT

Length: One to two days

Unit Sequence	Teacher Reflections
Post-Assessment This is a logical point in the unit to give an assessment that measures progress on the learning objectives explored thus far. Include traditional mathematics problems regarding ratio, proportion, geometric similarity, and indirect measurement. These problems should range from an algorithm in nature to an application-based algorithm. Other assessment items aligning with the generalizations or principles of the unit include but are not limited to the following: 1. Give students a handout with the word Relationships in the center. Prompt students to connect the following ideas in a way that makes sense for them: ratio, proportion, triangle similarity, indirect measurement. 2. How have people communicated culture and history through mathematics? Describe a situation today in which mathematical ideas can be used to "paint a picture" or "tell a story."	These problems can be found in mathematics textbooks. They are the same types of problems reflected in the pre-assessment. This provides an idea of individual student growth. It is important to note, however, that you will need to add in prompts related to the bigger concepts and generalizations or principles unraveled in this unit, because these are largely absent from traditional mathematics textbooks. Concept mapping is a useful way to have students continue to make purposeful connections between the knowledge or skills and the overarching big idea(s) and concepts. Are student seeing a larger picture in mathematics? Is a conceptual understanding evident? To look at student progress over time, refer to the opening brainstorm on relationships **(Resource 3.1: Think About It: What Is a Relationship?)**. How have students' understanding of relationships progressed? Are they able to connect the ideas of ratio, proportion, and so on to the larger generalization? Have students reflect on their own progress over time.
Continuation of Unit Under the umbrella of the primary unit principles or generalizations, this unit can easily be expanded to include topics such as perimeter and area of similar polygons and proportional segments.	

SUGGESTED READINGS

Silverstein, S. (1974). *Where the sidewalk ends*. New York: Harper & Row. Also available at
http://www.poemhunter.com/poem/one-inch-tall

Tomlinson, C. A. (2003). *Fulfilling the promise of the differentiated classroom*. Alexandria, VA:
ASCD.

RESOURCES

The following Resources can be found at the companion website for *Parallel Curriculum Units for Mathematics, Grades 6–12* at www.corwin.com/math6–12.

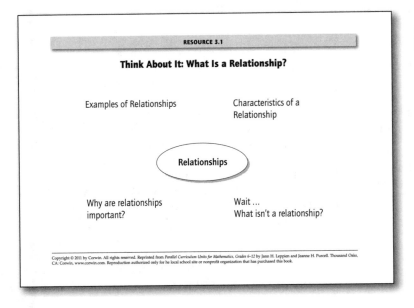

RESOURCE 3.1

Think About It: What Is a Relationship?

Examples of Relationships

Characteristics of a Relationship

Relationships

Why are relationships important?

Wait ...
What isn't a relationship?

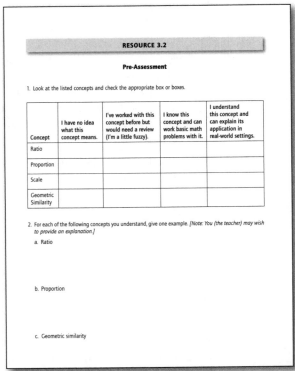

RESOURCE 3.2

Pre-Assessment

1. Look at the listed concepts and check the appropriate box or boxes.

Concept	I have no idea what this concept means.	I've worked with this concept before but would need a review (I'm a little fuzzy).	I know this concept and can work basic math problems with it.	I understand this concept and can explain its application in real-world settings.
Ratio				
Proportion				
Scale				
Geometric Similarity				

2. For each of the following concepts you understand, give one example. *[Note: You (the teacher) may wish to provide an explanation.]*

   a. Ratio

   b. Proportion

   c. Geometric similarity

RESOURCE 3.3

Pre-Assessment Key

The questions on this pre-assessment reflect (1) anticipated prerequisite knowledge, skills, and understandings students need coming into this unit, and (2) new knowledge, skills, and understandings in the unit. Students have most likely been exposed to the ideas of ratio and proportion at the middle school level. Because this unit builds from and expands these ideas, it is critical to know if students have a foundational understanding before proceeding with advanced learning. The majority of questions on this assessment aid in determining both individual entry points into the primary learning objectives and student interests. The questions represent a wide range of complexity from concrete or algorithmic to open-ended questions targeted at the larger conceptual framework. This pre-assessment aids in resource preparation and proactively constructing learning experiences that meet individual learning needs. Repeating these types of questions in both formative and summative assessments provides a measure of student growth and progress in relation to the primary learning objectives.

1. Look at the listed concepts and check the appropriate box or boxes.

Concept	I have no idea what this concept means.	I've worked with this concept before but would need a review (I'm a little fuzzy).	I know this concept and can work basic math problems with it.	I understand this concept and can explain its application in real-world settings.
Ratio				
Proportion				
Scale				
Geometric Similarity				

This question offers students the opportunity to self-report their own knowledge of key concepts in this unit and encourages them to be self-reflective in their own learning process. A quick glance over responses to this question provides some insight into the entry points of students.

RESOURCE 3.4

What Do You Know? Ratios and Proportions

1. On a scale from 1 (totally lost) to 10 (completely got it), I feel I am at a _____ with this material.

2. The one question I have is

3. Make a concept map or web that shows how the following terms connect:

   Relationship   Ratio   Proportion

4. In a class poll, you find that 10 students prefer chocolate ice cream and 22 students prefer vanilla. Given this situation, express a ratio that represents a
   a. part-to-part relationship and
   b. part-to-whole relationship.

5. Write four ratios that are proportional to $\frac{6}{9}$.

6. Hank's car can travel 90 miles on five gallons of fuel. How much fuel will his car consume if he travels 120 miles? What type of ratios are you dealing with?

7. How would you describe the idea of proportion to a student in fifth grade? Feel free to make an illustration, diagram, and so on.

8. How can ratios be a helpful mathematical tool?

9. How can you apply the mathematical thinking you have been doing (finding relationships, proportional reasoning, and so on) to your own life?

RESOURCE 3.5

Thinking Prompt

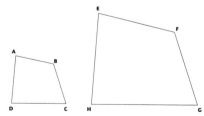

RESOURCE 3.6

Investigation: In Search of Similarity

Examples of Similarity

Quadrilateral ABCD is similar to quadrilateral EFGH . . .

and triangle ABC is similar to triangle DEF.

Performance Task: On the Grand Scale

The City Museum of Natural History is currently accepting proposals for an innovative exhibit featuring the Giza Pyramids. For one particular display, the curator would like museum visitors to gain a new perspective on the true magnitude of the Great Pyramid, which is the last surviving wonder of the ancient world. The display will feature a scale drawing of the Great Pyramid alongside another familiar object of your choice (monument, building, and so on). The primary goal of this display is to demonstrate how massive the Great Pyramid truly is in a way that visitors can appreciate. The overall design of this display is up to you. Proposals will be evaluated on how well the idea of geometric similarity is used in communicating an architectural perspective. The proposal should include

- a brief abstract (outline of your purpose and overall design process);
- a scale drawing on the paper provided to show the actual size of the display; and
- a short position paper addressing the following questions:
  - How did you use the idea of geometric similarity to construct your scale drawing (address relevant ratios, scale, and conditions of similarity)?
  - Why did you choose the object you did for comparison?
  - How well do you think you used the idea of geometric similarity to communicate a perspective?

Suggested Design Process (Nonlinear)

Understand the Problem or Task	Gather Needed or Relevant Information/Data
Communicate and Reflect	Analyze Possibilities
Construct and Modify	Decide on a Course of Action

Investigation: Justify It! Triangle Similarity

Situation at Hand: Four similarity "shortcuts or suspects" are claiming to be true. However, rumor has it that there is an imposter in the midst. The four shortcut suspects under investigation are AAA (or just A-A), SSS, SAS, and SSA. Using only your brain and the mathematical tools provided, construct a logical conclusion to this situation. *Justify it.*

Part I

Known: Polygons are similar *if and only if* the corresponding angles are congruent and the corresponding sides are proportional (equivalent ratios).

Unknown: Which shortcut suspects are true triangle similarity conditions?

Tools: Compass, ruler, straightedge, protractor, graph paper, tracing paper

Investigation 1: *Is AAA a Similarity Condition?*

If three sides of one triangle are proportional to three sides of another triangle, are the triangles similar? How do you know?

Investigation 2: *Is SSS a Similarity Condition?*

If three sides of one triangle are proportional to three sides of another triangle, are the triangles similar? How do you know?

Investigation 3: *Is SAS a Similarity Shortcut?*

If two pairs of corresponding sides are proportional and the included angles are congruent, are the two triangles similar? How do you know?

4

Quadratic Relationships

A Middle School Unit in Algebra, Grade 8

Carrie Heaney

INTRODUCTION TO THE UNIT

In this unit, students study the topic of quadratic relationships. Students identify the patterns that exist to create and represent quadratic relationships. Once students understand what makes up a quadratic relationship, they will learn to represent them mathematically, using graphs, tables, and equations. These representations help students realize the need for different methods in which they can solve problems that involve quadratic relationships.

In this unit, students are asked to "think like mathematicians." In the process of discovering what a quadratic relationship exemplifies, students analyze the world outside their classrooms to find quadratic relationships and then pose questions about these relationships that they will solve using the strategies they are taught in the unit. The goal of this unit is to move students from the mindset of "When am I ever going to use this?" to one where they can start to see the connections between the ideas that they are studying and the value that this mathematical knowledge provides them in solving real-world problems.

Quadratic relationships is a topic discussed in every Algebra 1 class; I believe, however, that students can lose the understanding of what they are learning and simply reduce the topic to a set of skills to perform a set of problems correctly if students are not taught the conceptual underpinnings prior to acquiring use of the procedural skills. When they later approach a similar problem that could be solved using a strategy that they have acquired in their learning of quadratic functions, they often are without an understanding that allows them to apply that learning to their new situation. This is why this unit was created: to give students the skills necessary to work with quadratic patterns and relationships as well as to give them an understanding of why they are using these skills so that transfer of learning can occur when solving unfamiliar problems that exist in our world.

The lessons in this unit are designed to address the Parallel Curriculum Model (PCM) parallels of Core Curriculum, Connections, and Practice. It is my belief that no unit can exist without starting at the Core Curriculum, so this parallel is present in almost every lesson. The decision to focus lessons using the Curriculum of Practice and the Curriculum of Connections comes from the belief stated earlier that the study of quadratics seems to be a turning point in learning where students' desires to understand the mathematics they are studying shifts to the memorization of "tricks" and "steps" so they can obtain the coveted correct answer. Unfortunately, this correct answer often comes without an understanding of the process they went through or what their answer represents.

Students begin this unit by discussing what the graph of a ball being tossed in the air might look like. This discussion leads students into the world of parabolas and all of their special characteristics (i.e., symmetry, vertex, zeros, maximum or minimum points). Students then search where they have encountered a parabola and capture that image digitally so they can use it to construct an understanding of the concepts. This discussion of graphs and tables is followed by some work with triangular numbers. Students then use the area of rectangles and squares to facilitate a discussion about the different forms that quadratic relationships take. Since these different forms require different solution strategies, students are able to start looking at the attributes of each form, the information that the form provides, and how best to find the answers they are looking for from the form in which they are working. The culminating instructional activity for this unit requires students to build and launch a rocket, to analyze the flight of the rocket using the strategies taught in this unit, to answer a set of questions I have posed, and to answer the questions they create for the activity.

Background for the Unit

It is expected that students have completed some course in pre-algebra, meaning that they have an understanding of representing situations with variables and equations as well as solving those equations for a given variable. It is also assumed that there has been prior study of algebraic patterns (i.e., linear and exponential relationships) and analysis of them via tables, graphs, and equations. A basic understanding of square roots is helpful as well, since students are asked to solve algebraic equations using square roots as one of their strategies. Students also will spend time working in small groups so a set of group norms and expectations should be determined to ensure student success when they set out to work in these groups.

One of the misconceptions that students have about quadratic relationships is that everything that follows a parabolic motion (i.e., projectiles) is a quadratic relationship. Since the effects of gravity on an object can be represented with a quadratic relationship, this is an easy misunderstanding to conclude. When teaching this unit, it is important that students be guided away from this misunderstanding by seeing a diverse set of scenarios that involve quadratic relationships.

This unit lends itself naturally to some extension work for students who reach an understanding of the topics being discussed more quickly than their counterparts do. For example, when discussing the topics of squaring and square roots as a part of the study of quadratic relationships, advanced students may benefit from instruction in the use of complex numbers. This will allow students who are ready to do so to start analyzing what happens when we try to find the square root of a negative number and then begin to work with ways to use this idea when they are working with quadratic relationships that involve complex solutions.

CONTENT FRAMEWORK

Organizing Concepts

Macroconcepts

M1: Change

M2: Systems

M3: Communication

Discipline-Specific Concepts

C1: Quadratic functions

C2: Quadratic graphs (axis of symmetry, maximum and minimum value, x-intercepts, vertex)

C3: Factoring trinomials

C4: Completing the square

C5: Zero product property

C6: Distributive property

Principles

P1: The way in which something changes predicts its true form.

P2: Change is inevitable; therefore, we need to be able to model change to understand it.

P3: Mathematical patterns may be communicated through situations, equations, graphs, and tables.

P4: Math is the language that quantifies the world.

P5: Graphs and tables are interrelated and effective ways to represent data.

P6: Equations are algebraic ways of representing the data in graphs, tables, and situations.

P7: Quadratic patterns of change (i.e., increasing or decreasing consecutive odd integers, squaring, second differences) can be used to model real-world situations.

P8: Mathematical strategies (i.e., completing the square, factoring trinomials, distributive property, solving equations using square roots) provide an approach for problem solving.

P9: Relationships and functions are the way that mathematicians represent patterns.

P10: The patterns involved in a relationship indicate the type of function we are working with.

National Standards, National Council for Teachers of Mathematics

SD1: Understand patterns, relationships, and functions

SD2: Represent and analyze mathematical situations and structures using algebraic symbols

SD3: Use mathematical models to represent and understand quantitative relationships

SD4: Analyze change in various contexts

SD5: Apply and adapt a variety of appropriate strategies to solve problems

SD6: Make and investigate mathematical conjectures

SD7: Communicate mathematical thinking coherently and clearly to peers, teachers, and others

SD8: Use the language of mathematics to express mathematical ideas precisely

SD9: Recognize and use connections among mathematical ideas

SD10: Recognize and apply mathematics in contexts outside mathematics

SD11: Create and use representations to organize, record, and communicate mathematical ideas

SD12: Select, apply, and translate among mathematical representations to solve problems

SD13: Use technology to solve mathematical problems

Skills

S1: Identify quadratic relationships from tables, graphs, and equations

S2: Create tables, graphs, and equations for quadratic relationships

S3: Use tables and graphs to make predictions about a quadratic relationship

S4: Use tables, graphs, and equations to solve problems involving quadratic relationships

S5: Move fluidly between the different representations of a quadratic relationship

S6: Determine the appropriate representation of a quadratic function to help solve problems involving quadratics

S7: Identify equivalent quadratic equations

S8: Identify quadratic equations written in factored and expanded form

S9: Write a quadratic equation to match a graph or table of data

S10: Use the distributive property to solve problems involving quadratic relationships

S11: Multiply binomials using the distributive property

S12: Identify the features of a quadratic graph (max/min, zeros, vertex, line of symmetry, y-intercept)

S13: Predict the features of a graph from its equation (max/min, zeros, vertex, line of symmetry, y-intercept)

S14: Compare quadratic relationships and their patterns with the patterns of other functions explored earlier (linear, exponential)

S15: Solve quadratic functions using a variety of strategies

S16: Complete the square

S17: Derive the quadratic equation

S18: Use the discriminant to determine the number of solutions for a quadratic relationship

S19: Factor quadratic expressions

S20: Find the second differences of a table

S21: Make quadratic graphs and tables using a graphing calculator

S22: Identify a quadratic pattern of change from a table, graph, equation, and situation

S23: Solve quadratic equations in the forms $x^2 = k$ and $ax^2 + bx + c = 0$

S24: Read, create, and interpret graphs of quadratic inequalities

S25: Use the quadratic formula to solve problems involving quadratic relationships

ASSESSMENTS

Assessments in this unit will be used to provide different types of information to you as well as to the students about what they are learning and where they may need further instruction.

Pre-Assessments

The pre-assessment for this unit is a paper-and-pencil test where students are asked to use the strategies to solve the problems they will encounter in this unit. These problems will be naked math problems, problems without context (e.g., solve $f(x) = x^2 + 5x - 14$ for x), so that I can see if students know the strategies that I am presenting to them in this unit. Students are given the paper-and-pencil test because it will allow me to see quickly whether they have mastered a strategy. In addition to these problems, students also will receive a list of questions about the essential understandings for the unit so that they can reveal what they already know about these ideas.

Students will be given half of the class period to complete the pre-assessment problems. Since this is a pre-assessment, students are reminded that it is completely fine to not have the "correct answer" and that the process that is valued here is the thoughts they are putting on their paper. Once they have completed the problems, they will grade the assessment based on the answer key provided. As students grade the problem, they will fill out a scale next to the problem that indicates how comfortable they are with the topic. If a student skips a problem, he will indicate that on the scale as well. This comfort scale will provide teachers with insight into the perceptions students hold regarding their level of confidence. The comfort scale provides a small snapshot of the students' thinking at that particular time so that you can use the information more effectively. Having students identify their comfort level gives you the opportunity to assist individual students. If students indicate that they are really comfortable with the topic or task and have the correct answer, then you can probe what it is they really understand. Often I encounter students who know a process but do not understand why it works; this knowledge guides the kinds of questions I use to assess their understanding. Also, the comfort scale gives me insight into whether or not my students were making educated guesses or just got lucky in their responses.

After students correct the papers, they will turn them in to you and work in pairs to write down their ideas and comments about the essential questions. By having the students work in pairs, even though each is individually responsible for her own answers, provides an opportunity for them to jump-start their thinking as well as to reinforce the cooperative learning expectations that exist in this unit. At the end of the unit, these comments and ideas will be returned to the students with an additional request to add any new thoughts or understanding about their learning. This will help them to see how their knowledge and level of understanding have changed over the course of the unit.

Formative Assessments

Within this unit, there will be many formative assessments that are used during the lessons. I will be listening to the conversations that students have with each other, as well as listening to the class as a whole, to identity any misconceptions, in-depth understandings, or unusual thoughts and approaches about the topic that is being discussed that day. As a way of monitoring and keeping track of the information that I gain from these conversations, I use a clipboard with every student's name listed. This allows me to jot down thoughts and ideas that need to be addressed later. For example, if I feel a student has a misconception that was not cleared up during instruction, I make a note to touch base with him during the next class; if there are many students with that misconception, I provide a different lesson to reinforce some skills that were taught. If I notice a student who is grasping a concept quickly, I also make note of it and make sure that I offer a more challenging approach to the concept at hand, or change my approach with that student completely, depending on what my other assessments indicate.

In several lessons, students are given "ticket-out-the-door" assessments. These assessments consist of either a problem or a question that students need to answer before they can exit the class. Their answers are their ticket out of class that day. In some lessons, the "ticket-out-the-door" assessments are more of a conversation between the student and you. Students are asked to list at least two "ahas" that they had during that day, as well as at least one question that they still have about the topic. These questions and "ahas" will be used in the opening of the next class to start some conversations; you might also alter the course of the instruction based on what specific instruction the students need.

In other lessons, students are given an equation or situation that needs to be solved using the method(s) for solving quadratics that were discussed during the lesson. If a student cannot solve these problems, then she is expected to write down a specific question that will help her solve the problem. This question automatically creates an opportunity for dialogue between you and the student that can be addressed either quickly at the end of class or in more depth at another time, depending on the type of question asked. These quick problems provide you with the type of information to determine whether the instruction on a particular topic needs to be revisited or to identify potential misunderstandings in the homework that is assigned. These misconceptions can be discussed by the whole class or individually.

In this unit, two traditional 10-point quizzes are administered. These assessments serve a couple of different purposes. For starters, they build in a sort of benchmark checklist for students that allows them to see if they have acquired mathematical understandings, in the depth necessary, to be successful by the end of the unit. I often find that students need these checkpoint quizzes so they can obtain a reality check of what they know in an environment that is informative but not totally risk free. The risk-free environment requires students to ask questions of you, the teacher, but sometimes not of themselves. When students see a quiz score that they don't like, it prompts them to ask the questions that they have not asked before and provides you with information about their comfort levels with a topic. After both of these quizzes, students are given workdays to complete their unit projects; if the quizzes indicate to you that some students need additional help, you can work with students individually or in small groups to provide additional assistance. The first quiz is designed to show student understanding of how to find the characteristics of a quadratic graph that were discussed in earlier lessons; the second quiz occurs toward the end of the unit and assesses student understanding of the different ways to solve quadratic equations.

Mid-Unit Project Assessment

Solving quadratic equations and understanding which method to use are very abstract concepts in this unit. At this point in the instructional process, this is a good place to stop and have students do some thinking about these ideas so they can acquire skills and strategies that they will use within this unit, as well as within their future units of study. In order to help students create some meaning out of what we are working on, you need to ask them to complete one of three tasks suggested below. Each task requires students to show an understanding of solving quadratic equations, and to indicate when each strategy is most useful and appropriate. Students will select one of three tasks to complete:

- *Practical Task.* Create a problem that you would solve by each method and explain how to solve that problem.
- *Analytical Task.* Create a "Dummies Guide" to solving quadratic equations, highlight each type of solution, and explain how to do it and when is the best time to use each type of solution.
- *Creative Task.* Create a game that involves using each type of solving quadratics as a benchmark for winning the game.

Post-Assessments

There are several post-assessment projects that accompany this unit. I believe that since the material has been provided to students in numerous ways, it is essential to provide them with a number of ways to show us what they have mastered. The first post-assessment is a traditional paper-and-pencil assessment, much like the pre-assessment, where students will be given several types of problems that can be solved using the strategies taught in this unit. In a math class, students are asked to take these types of tests: I believe I do my students a disservice by not preparing them for this part of their educational career. It is also my belief, however, that if you were to ask a mathematician who is working in the field when his last paper-and-pencil test was administered, he would probably shake his head and laugh. Thus, the second form of post-assessment that students will be asked to perform is a task in which students write an equation that represents the height of a rocket's flight and then use this equation to answer questions about the flight of the rocket. I provide several questions that they must answer, and also ask students to pose a few questions of their own for which they would like answers. In addition to finding the answers to these questions, students will be asked to explain why they selected their particular strategy. The idea behind this assessment is to have students approach what they have learned through the eyes of a practitioner who would have to solve this problem. Throughout the unit, I have asked students to look for places to use these skills, so it seems only appropriate that I back my requests with an opportunity for students to show me, through such a task, what they know.

Thanks to the hobby-shop industry, building model rockets can be as easy or as difficult as you want and as expensive or inexpensive as you need. I have students work in groups of four to build and launch their rockets. Students are placed in groups based on their understanding of the concepts in this unit and according to their mathematical learning styles. Placing students based on their understanding of the unit topics provides you with an opportunity to differentiate the questions as well as the rockets that students are given, since different rockets require different levels of skill to build and fly. Once the rockets are ready to fly, the groups videotape the launch and then analyze the footage so that they can write an equation to represent the height of the rocket's flight over time, as well as answer the other questions that they pose about their rockets. If budget permits, I would recommend allowing every group two launches for each rocket; if that is not an option, however, I recommend having a few extra rocket engines available in case of glitches that may occur in the taping of the flight. The rubric for this project will involve how accurately a student's equations represent the flight of her rocket, a detailed look at the graph and table that represents the flight of that rocket, and a reflection about how she was able to write and solve an equation for this activity.

The third form of post-assessment for this unit is a reflection about the essential understandings that are presented to students in this unit. On the pre-assessment for this unit, students are asked to respond to several questions that address the principles for this unit. As we work through the unit, students are asked to add comments about these understandings in their mathematical learning journals. At the end of the unit, students are given their original comments from the pre-assessment and asked to use a different-colored marker to add additional ideas based on what they have come to understand. They can change any of their original ideas based on their new knowledge. This helps them to see how their understanding has changed over the course of this unit.

Assessing the Major Concepts in This Unit

The major concepts that are addressed in this unit are change, communication, and systems. The way that I induce the understanding of these concepts is to ask students to reflect on the ideas as they arise in the activities and lessons. The questions are asked individually to students as they reach a point in their thinking where it is appropriate, or they are posed to the whole class as they are coming to an understanding as a group. Often the whole-class discussions are recorded in their math journals or as ticket-out-the-door assessments, where students record their thoughts and give them to me as they leave the class that day. Often the ticket-out-the-door responses will be used as a warm-up activity the next day, when I post some of the class responses and ask the students to reflect on how those answers coincide or fit within their own answers. These responses are recorded on their warm-up sheets or class notes, and are discussed as a whole class before we start the lesson for that day.

My recommendation to teachers who use this unit would be to use the following question prompts to assess student understanding of these concepts:

Change

- How does the way a relationship changes indicate the type of problem you're working with?
- Can the way a relationship changes be used to make future problems easier to solve?
- How does a pattern of change indicate the type of relationship you're working with?
- The world around us is not static. How does the fact that things are always changing affect the study of mathematics?
- In mathematics, we classify change with relationships, that is, linear, nonlinear, exponential, quadratic, and so on. How is change classified outside mathematics?

Communication

- How do you think mathematically?
- How can you work with others who think differently about math than you do?
- There are many ways to say the same things in mathematics. How does this play into your need to understand a problem's solution in more than one way?
- Equivalence is an essential mathematical understanding. How has that idea been seen in today's class discussion?
- Today we've looked at multiple representations of a quadratic relationship. Why is it important to be able to see the same relationships in many different ways?
- How can you use the patterns you see to mathematically explain the world around you?

Systems

- Mathematicians all have different backgrounds and means to communicate their ideas. What systems are in place in the discipline of mathematics to guarantee that mathematicians understand each other?
- Can pattern recognition provide shortcuts to solving problems?
- How do we determine which situations lend themselves to a particular method of solution?

UNIT SEQUENCE, DESCRIPTION, AND TEACHER REFLECTIONS

LESSON 4.1: MATH LEARNING STYLES

Length: One day

Unit Sequence	Teacher Reflections
Concepts M3	At the beginning of the unit, give a math learning styles assessment to the students (**Resource 4.1: Math Learning Styles Worksheet**). The idea behind this lesson is for students to understand themselves as learners in order to function in their most efficient style. Make sure that students know that they can fit into more than one learning style: they need to choose the style of expression that they use most frequently.
Standards SD5, SD7	
Guiding Questions 1. How do I think mathematically? 2. How can I work with others who think differently about math than I do?	
Introduction, and Teaching and Learning Experiences *Learning Styles* Provide students with definitions of the four mathematical learning styles listed on **Resource 4.1: Math Learning Styles Worksheet.** Ask them to identify which definition of style best fits their learning style most of the time. Have students answer the following questions on the back of the sheet: 1. What really helps you learn math? 2. What is least helpful to you when learning math? Once they have completed their responses, ask them to return this handout to you.	During this assessment, students may become very conscious of the groups they may be placed in during instruction based on their responses. They may want to change their answers based on their friends' responses. By collecting the sheets before the *Grouping Based on Style* activity, you will have an unaltered view of the students, even if they alter their view of themselves. Once students have a list of what works and what doesn't, it is important for them to know that this doesn't mean they are excused from having to perform in this style. The assessment is designed to help students identify their strengths as well as to develop strategies for working outside their comfort areas when necessary.

Unit Sequence	Teacher Reflections
Grouping Based on Style Using the students' responses to this assessment, have them report to the designated location in the room that matches their style. (There should be four locations, one for each of the four mathematical learning styles listed on **Resource 4.1: Math Learning Styles Worksheet**.) Once students are grouped based on the math learning style identified, ask them to share their answers to the assessment with each other and then create a list on large chart paper of the strategies or methods they believe assist them in their learning. In these groups, students share their responses, and look for the similarities and differences in these styles. Once all learner profiles are shared, have students respond to the following questions in their math journals: 1. How do I think mathematically? 2. How can I work with others who think differently about math than I do? 3. What new understandings have I gained about myself as a mathematical learner?	Be sure that students are paying attention to the learner style and not to the individuals in that group. A student may decide she cannot work with a group based on a personal conflict with an individual and so not benefit from the purpose of this activity. Be sure that all learning styles are represented in this conversation. Make sure, also, that no discussions are directed at any one individual. Explain to students that we often do not get to choose who we work with in life, so inevitably we need to find ways to work with each other.
Closure After students complete their journal entries, lead a whole-group discussion on strategies that can respectfully solve potential style conflicts and ensure positive communication.	This discussion serves to establish a classroom environment where learning profile differences are respected; it offers students an opportunity to learn strategies for resolving potential group conflict based on style differences.

LESSON 4.2: THROWING A BALL

Length: One day

Unit Sequence	Teacher Reflections
Concepts M1, C1, C2	
Principles P1, P2, P3, P4, P5	
Standards SD3, SD4, SD7, SD12	
Skills S1, S2, S3, S4, S5, S24	
Guiding Questions 1. What about the motion of a ball makes it mathematical? 2. How is the motion of the ball seen in the graph and the table? 3. How do you mathematically describe the change in the height of the ball's flight?	This lesson is being taught through the Core Parallel. In this lesson, students are exploring the basic vocabulary and characteristics of a quadratic function.
Introduction, and Teaching and Learning Experiences *Introduction* In this lesson, students are exposed to a simple quadratic pattern that requires them to start thinking about the graphs of a quadratic function. Begin by standing in the front of the classroom and tossing a ball into the air. Ask the class to describe the path of the ball as it travels and to identify anything they see that they believe is important. As students describe the path of the ball, use these questions to prompt further discussion: 1. How high did the ball start from the ground? 2. How high did the ball go? 3. Was there a point where the ball stopped? 4. Why did the path of the ball eventually decrease?	Have the following materials available to students: a ball for each group, large chart graph paper, stopwatches, and math journals.

Unit Sequence	Teacher Reflections

Flight of a Ball: Group Activity
 	
After this discussion, group students into three member teams based on their earlier identified preferred math learning style. Ask each group to create a table and graph of the height of the ball's flight over time; they will transfer this table and graph to chart paper so that it can be discussed by the whole class when all groups are finished with the task. Hand out the **Resource 4.2: Flight of a Ball: Group Activity** worksheet for students to record their responses.
 	
    When all groups have finished, have them place their charts on the wall. Have one member of each group explain how they came up with their graphs and tables. As students are explaining their work, be sure to have them address the following questions that are included on the **Resource 4.3: Flight of a Ball: Reflections** worksheet:
 	
1. How did you know where to start your table?
 	
2. Why did you choose the time intervals you chose?
 	
3. Do the graph and table increase or decrease?
 	
4. What was the graph's maximum height?
 	
5. Does this graph cross the *x*-axis? Where and what does this represent or tell us?
 	
6. Does the graph cross the *y*-axis? Where and what does it represent?
 	
    Then have students return to their groups and discuss how the table and graph of this relationship are related; and how they can see where the ball starts, reaches its highest point, and stops in their table and graph.
    Once students have answered the questions in **Resource 4.3: Flight of a Ball: Reflections**, ask them these questions:
 	
    Which form of representation—the graph or the table—is easier for you to use?
 	
    How do you illustrate change?
 	
As a whole group, discuss the answers to these questions. Explain to students that these key points have mathematical names that they should know: *x*-intercept, maximum point,
	Leave the directions for the table and graph open-ended so you can adjust the difficulty level of the problem to fit each group's readiness levels.
	
	    Place these questions on the board to guide group conversations.
	    Many students will have a *v*-shaped graph instead of the *u* shape that is a parabola. Make sure that students understand why a *v* shape does not work. (You might be able to offer a nice extension to students to find out what mathematical function the *v*-shaped graph represents.)
	
	    It is important to help students to see that the graphs and tables are ways of showing what happens in the situation without having to re-create the situation every time they are trying to analyze the situation, and that each form shows the same information differently. This will start to lead students to thinking about the representation that is the most appropriate for the solution they are seeking.
	    On the **Resource 4.4: Flight of a Ball: Post-Class Discussion**, it is important to assess student understanding of the macroconcept of change more directly by analyzing how students address the following question: How is the change you have seen in the flight of the ball alike or different from other mathematical relationships (i.e., linear, exponential) you have worked with this year?

Unit Sequence	Teacher Reflections
y-intercept, and axis of symmetry. Have students sketch in their journals the graph and the table, reminding them to make sure to identify all of these ideas for future reference. Then ask students to work in their groups to identify a situation that could be represented by a table that would create a parabola that had a minimum point. Discuss these situations as a class and ask students to decide if they agree or disagree with these situations. Hand out the **Resource 4.4: Flight of a Ball: Post-Class Discussion** worksheet to record their responses.	*Ascending Intellectual Demand* As students are mastering the idea of the graph predicting height over time, you could ask students to think about what it would mean if we shaded the inside of the graph. Students will have had experience with linear inequalities in prior units, so they should be able to communicate that everything under the curve would be a solution to the problem. Ask the students to try to think of a situation where a graph like this could be thought of as an inequality. This will be a struggle for students, and will not be a question that is asked of every student.
Closure To conclude today's lesson, ask students to sketch the graph and create the table for the parabola with a minimum point. This assessment serves as a ticket out the door and provides you with data to determine the degree of student understanding. *Homework* Ask students to complete the following task and to return the product to class the next day. Distribute **Resource 4.5: Homework Slip** to remind students of their assignment. The task is as follows: You are to find a parabola somewhere in your surroundings. Take a picture of it with a digital camera or camera phone. If a camera is not available, draw a picture of that parabola and bring it to class tomorrow.	This is a quick assessment tool to use with students at the closure of a lesson. This provides you with evidence of student understanding on an individual level.

LESSON 4.3: PRE-ASSESSMENT

Length: One class period

Unit Sequence	Teacher Reflections
Concepts M1, M2, M3, C1–C6	These concepts are being pre-assessed in this lesson.
Principles P1, P3, P4, P5, P6, P8, P9, P10	Initial understanding of these principles is being pre-assessed.
Standards SD1–SD9, SD12	These standards are being pre-assessed.
Skills S1, S2, S5, S8, S10, S12, S13, S15, S16, S23, S25	These skills are being pre-assessed.
Introduction, and Teaching and Learning Experiences *Paper-and-Pencil Pre-Assessment, Part I* The paper-and-pencil pre-assessment for this unit includes two parts (**Resource 4.6: Paper-and-Pencil Pre-Assessment, Part I**; and **Resource 4.7: Responding to Essential Understanding Pre-Assessment, Part II**). The first assessment is a paper-and-pencil response where students are asked to use the strategies from this unit to solve the problems they will encounter in this unit.	Normally, a pre-assessment is given at the beginning of a unit. Since the first two lessons in the unit can be easily differentiated to meet students' needs, however, I decided to have students take the pre-assessment after Day 2 in an effort to provide them with more time to gather their parabola pictures and to build in a day that allows for technology difficulties. The rationale behind this test is to help guide my instruction so that I am not holding students back by discussing things they are already familiar with, and to identify times when I will be able to differentiate instruction for my students based on the skills that they bring to this unit prior to instruction. Students are given the paper-and-pencil pre-assessment so that I can quickly see whether they have already mastered a strategy. Having students identify their comfort level gives me the opportunity to work with students at the level of readiness they have of this topic. If they indicate that they are really comfortable with a topic and have demonstrated the correct answer, then I can probe into what it is they really know. Often I find students will know a process but not understand why it works; that knowledge will allow me focus on the kind of questions I will ask a particular student during the unit. Also, it gives me insight into whether they are making educated guesses or if they just got lucky in the response.

Unit Sequence	Teacher Reflections
Responding to Essential Understandings Pre-Assessment, Part II The second part of the pre-assessment requires students to respond to a list of the big ideas from the unit that serves as the framework for student understandings that are essential for ensuring student mastery.	Part II of the pre-assessment requires students to explain what they already know about the essential ideas for the unit. This provides me with assessment data about what they already understand. By asking them to revise these explanations throughout the unit, I can gather further evidence of their understanding as they work with concepts that are more advanced. At the end of the unit, students return to their responses to further refine their comments by adding any new insights they have about these ideas and to summarize how their knowledge has changed over the course of the unit. As the unit progresses, you should post student comments about the essential understandings or principles identified for this unit on chart paper hung around the room. As new discoveries are made, concepts will be added to the list. Additionally, students will have a page for each essential understanding or principle in their notebooks, which will serve as a study guide or thought guide they can return to at the end of the unit.
Closure When students are finished with these pre-assessments, they will be allowed to download or scan the pictures of parabolas that they were asked to find as homework in Lesson 4.2.	

LESSON 4.4: THE MATH CURSE: NOW I SEE PARABOLAS EVERYWHERE!

Length: Two class periods

Unit Sequence	Teacher Reflections
Concepts C2	
Principles P3, P5, P6	
Standards SD1, SD2, SD6, SD10, SD11	
Skills S1, S2, S3, S12, S14, S15, S22	
Guiding Questions 1. What about parabolas makes them occur naturally in our surroundings? 2. Why do human beings look for ways to understand the world around them? 3. How does the study of mathematics lend itself to explaining the world around us?	This lesson is being taught using the parallel of Curriculum of Connections. Allowing students to look for their own parabolas allows them to make connections to the math we are studying and to the world around them. The properties of a parabola no longer are part of some strange picture their teacher provides them, but are real parts of real shapes that they are seeing in the world around them.
Introduction, and Teaching and Learning Experiences *Introduction* Read aloud *The Math Curse* by Jon Scieszka (1995). Ask students if the ideas in this book illustrate how they feel about parabolas. Follow this discussion with the following questions: Once you started looking, were you able to see them everywhere or were they oblivious to my math curse? Did you have a hard time seeing parabolas in the world around you? *Sharing of Parabolas* Next, ask students to share where they found their parabolas. Project or present the pictures that students have brought in from the homework assignment completed in Lesson 4.3. Students should have submitted all pictures on the day of the pre-assessment so that you can make sure they were scanned or downloaded and ready for this lesson.	This short story pokes fun at a teacher who puts a math curse on her student: as a result, this student sees math everywhere. The story provides a good starting point for students to start their discussion about all of the places that they found parabolas. It is a good idea to have some spare pictures of parabolas; it is inevitable that either technology or something else will prevent students from having a parabola to share with the class.

Unit Sequence	Teacher Reflections
Students will be working in pairs on this activity in the computer lab. Because the students will be submitting their parabolas the day before, you will have time to look them over prior to this class so that the pairing of students can be decided based on which parabolas are the least alike.	Students are *paired up* for this activity for many different reasons. First, it will give them the opportunity to see more than one parabola in depth. Second, it will provide you with an opportunity to differentiate the lesson. The students can be placed together because their parabolas are different, in an effort to bring about discussions about what they see and why the scales for each parabola need to be so different. Your role during this time is to encourage students to think about their parabolas by asking the questions mentioned in the lesson. You might work with students who might need more support by giving them similar parabolas in an effort to reinforce the ideas without too much extraneous information. Third, it is always nice to have two students who can work together when they are trying an activity that involves technology. Students can problem solve together, providing time for you to circulate around the computer lab to listen to student conversations.
Creating the Coordinate Grid Distribute the **Resource 4.8: Creating the Coordinate Grid** handout to students. Have students read and discuss the directions for this activity before they begin working on the computers. When students are creating the coordinate grid that they are going to link to their picture, use the following questions to prompt their thinking:	Students need access to the following technology: computers, MS Excel software, computer projectors, scanners, or document cameras.
1. Do you know anything about the parabola that will help you with this task? 2. Does it make sense to start the graph at the origin? 3. Does the scale on your *x*- and *y*-axes match the situation? 4. Why are the scales so different for the parabolas you are working with?	Students may not have a story that goes with their parabola so they may not be able to answer specific questions. However, you can still ask them to think about the graph they are creating and inquire whether it should be placed in any quadrant other than Quadrant I. They will have some concept of the size of the original parabola that they saw, and therefore should be able to use that to determine their scale for the axes.

Unit Sequence	Teacher Reflections
Once students have created their graphs, ask them to find the following points on their graph: x-intercept, y-intercept, minimum/maximum point, and line of symmetry. In addition to finding these points, ask the students to describe what these points tell them about the parabola they are working with. Have each pair of students share one of their graphs and the points that they have identified with the class. Students should explain the points on the graph and what they mean in terms of the graph.	Ask students who are really struggling with this idea to give you a brief description of the parabola; putting things into their own words will help them to set the stage for the graph. If they do not have a story that goes with the graph once students identify these points, their descriptions of the points will be much more generic. You can still prompt them to think about the situation, however. For example, if they have taken a picture of a parabola that they see in the supports of their patio, ask them why a carpenter might be interested in knowing where the x-intercepts are. Just because there isn't a story does not mean that they cannot put some frame of reference to the topic they are looking at. Ask students who are really struggling with this idea to give you a brief description of the parabola. Putting ideas into their own words will help "set the stage" for the creation of their graph.
Closure To close this lesson, assign the following homework questions by distributing the **Resource 4.9: The Parabola Curse: Homework Assignment** handout: 1. What about parabolas make them occur naturally in our surroundings? 2. Why do human beings look for ways to understand the world around them? 3. How does the study of mathematics lend itself to explaining the world around us? 4. What about projectile motion makes it mathematical? 5. How can quadratic relationships be used to describe the change in a projectile's height?	Have students read the directions for this homework assignment. Encourage them to ask additional questions that may support their thinking as they respond to this assignment individually.

LESSON 4.5: QUADRATIC PATTERNS

Length: Two class periods

Unit Sequence	Teacher Reflections
Concepts M1, M3, C6	
Principles P1, P2, P3, P6, P7, P9, P10	
Standards SD1, SD2, SD5, SD6, SD8, SD9, SD11	
Skills S1, S2, S3, S7, S8, S9, S10, S20	
Guiding Questions 1. How can I use the patterns I see to mathematically explain the world around me? 2. How does a pattern of change indicate the type of relationship I'm working with? 3. Can pattern recognition provide shortcuts to solving problems? 4. How can I generalize a recursive situation?	This lesson is being taught using the Core Parallel. The purpose of this lesson is to allow students the opportunity to look at some quadratic patterns and write equations using their prior knowledge about recognizing patterns for a table or picture.
Introduction, and Teaching and Learning Experiences *Introduction* Explain to students that there are many different types of quadratic patterns that they will encounter. Because quadratic patterns occur readily in nature, many mathematicians have taken the time to identify these patterns and create pictures or representations of them that allow the person studying the pattern to work with the numbers in a visual and kinesthetic way. Today, we are going to look at some of these patterns in an effort to help build and deepen our understanding of quadratic patterns of change.	

Unit Sequence	Teacher Reflections

Learning Task
 	
Distribute Figurate Numbers Task Cards (**Resources 4.10: Figurate Numbers Task Card: Triangular Numbers, 4.11: Figurate Numbers Task Card: Square Numbers, and 4.12: Figurate Numbers Task Card: Rectangular Numbers**) to the students, with one copy of each resource going to each student.
 	
Ask the students to complete the following tasks:
 	
1. Draw Figures 0, 4, and 5 based on Figures 1, 2, and 3 you were given.
 	
2. Make a table of the figure number, n, and the total number of dots in that number, t.
 	
3. Use the figures to write an expression that relates the figure number, n, to the total number of dots in the shape, t.
 	
4. Use your equation to predict the number of dots in Shape 100.
 	
5. Create a written description or guide to see the pattern in your shape that inspired your equation.
 	
Have the groups who had the same patterns get together and compare or edit their equations and methods for writing the equations. While the students are working in these combined groups, ask them to look at the following things:
 	
1. Did everyone draw the same Shapes 4 and 5? If not, discuss who has the correct shapes.
 	
2. How would you describe the creation of Shapes 4 and 5?
 	
3. Does everyone have the same values for total number of tiles in their tables? If not, discuss who is correct.
 	
4. What was the total number of dots in Shape 100?
 	
5. Compare equations for the total number of dots, t.
 	
   • Are the equations the same? If not, are they equivalent?
   • How can you see your equation in the shapes?
	The tasks on the cards are the same for each group, but the patterns that the students are asked to analyze are at different levels of difficulty. Have two different groups analyze the same pattern so that you have the potential for students to write equivalent expressions to represent the pattern and create a point of discussion for the lesson. Even if the groups write the same equation, they still will most likely have thought of the process in different ways so the discussion of their process will be rich.
	
	The groups for this activity should be based on ability; if you find that a group easily completes a task, do not hesitate to give that group a different number pattern that will challenge that group to write an equivalent expression for the pattern they have as a means to extend members' thinking.
	
	As students work to write their equations, they often initially see the pattern recursively. Recursive equations are often easy for students to describe verbally, but harder for them to describe algebraically. Encourage the students to write a general equation: in order for a recursive equation to predict the total number of dots in the next shape, they need to know the previous number of dots and that can lead to an inefficient method for calculating the number of dots in Shape 100.
	
	If students are having a hard time seeing the pattern or if they are becoming too reliant on their tables (for some students the tables will reinforce the recursive thinking), encourage them to create the shapes using color or to actually build the shapes using sticker dots or M&Ms, or to draw them using the squares on graph paper.
	
	As the students are working in their combined groups, it is important for them to discuss how they see Shapes 4 and 5 being created. This process is often where they start to see their equations; if they see different ways of creating the shapes, they will likely see different equations.
	
	As students are seeing that they have written equivalent expressions, it is usually the distributive property that students are using that allows them to algebraically manipulate the equations to show their equivalence. It is important at this stage to be sure to give the process its name and guarantee that students are aware that they are using the distributive property to complete these problems.

Unit Sequence	Teacher Reflections
Creating Posters	Encourage students to use color in the posters, because it is a way to allow the pattern to be seen in the picture as well as it is represented in the equation. This will allow students to see the patterns more easily during the gallery walk.

Creating Posters

Have the students return to their original groups and create a poster for their figurate number. Their poster needs to include all of the steps that they took; the presentation must be in an organized manner, so they can easily be read and interpreted by the rest of the class.

Poster requirements include these:

1. Draw Figures 0, 4, and 5 based on Figures 1, 2, and 3 you were given.

2. Make a table of the figure number, n, and the total number of dots in figure number, t.

3. Use the figures to write an expression that relates the figure number, n, to the total number of dots in the shape, t.

4. Use your equation to predict the number of dots in Shape 100.

5. Create a written description or guide to seeing the pattern in your shape that inspired your equation.

Have the students place a copy of their shape task into their math journals.

Gallery Walk

Once the posters have been created, post them around the room and have the students do a gallery walk. Give students sticky notes to use as they conduct the gallery walk. For each poster they view, they should identify one positive thought, one question, and one piece of constructive feedback. They should write each thought, question, or feedback on a sticky note and place it on the poster.

Gallery Walk Protocol

- *Quiet.* You are analyzing and giving feedback to these groups. It is something that should be done quietly. You can discuss with your group members as you work, but it should be done as a whisper so as not to disturb the analysis of other groups.
- *Sticky Notes.* Be sure that your feedback is constructive. Make sure that your comments help the group make the posters and their discussion better. This means if you like their colors, tell them why so they don't change them. If you find that something distracts from the poster, tell them why so they know what to address if they were to change it.

The gallery walk allows students the opportunity to see all of the work and thought processes of the other groups in a shorter period of time than just presenting to the class. It also allows the students the opportunity to move around the room.

The gallery walk protocols are important: making sure that the students know what they are looking for as they walk around will help them to get the most from the gallery walk. It will also allow them to be more productive, since the environment of the room will be one of analysis and structure.

A great way to build accountability into this activity is to give each group a different-colored sticky note. This allows you to quickly glance at each poster and see if each group has responded to all of the posters.

Unit Sequence	Teacher Reflections
After the gallery walk, allow the groups to return to their posters and look at their feedback, comments, and questions. Ask the students to think about the feedback. Can they use it? If they were to do this activity again, what would they keep? What would they change? Why? Then ask the students to address the questions that were left on their posters, since they will be asked to answer or discuss them during the class discussion. Then, as a whole class, have a discussion about the different patterns that the students observed. Ask the students the following questions: • Were there any similarities that you saw as you looked at the patterns? • As you looked at each pattern and its equations, was there anything about a particular pattern that would have helped you when you were working on your *own* pattern? • For the patterns that were the same, were there any differences in the way that the problem was approached? • Were these patterns quadratic? How do you know? Be sure to allow the groups to address the questions that were left on their posters as you go through this discussion at each poster. After the gallery walk, have students record the patterns and equations that they were not responsible for into their math journals.	During this discussion is a good time to remind students about factored and expanded forms of equations. For example, if a group wrote the equation $t = n(n + 1)$, it would be a great time to discuss how that equation is equivalent to $t = n^2 + n$. It is also a great time to explain how the two equations really represent two different ways of seeing the pattern being built. The first equation discusses how the length and width of the rectangle changes, and the second equation focuses on seeing a square in the pattern and how it become a rectangle by adding another row that is the same length as the shape number. Also, during this discussion be sure to go back to the fact that the patterns are quadratic functions, and then ask the students to explain how they know this. They should be able to address the superscript "2" in the equations and the second differences in the table. The students' record of the patterns and equations after the gallery walk should not be too detailed. The students just need a quick sketch of Shapes 1, 2, and 3; the equation; and any thoughts that they had about that pattern. Since they have gone through the process in detail, the purpose of this information is just to provide a resource to the students that they can return to as a reference.
Closure As students are leaving the room, ask them to fill out **Resource 4.13: 3–2–1 Exit Slip Worksheet.** In this task, they are asked to identify three things that they understand about writing equations from patterns, two things that they need clarification on, and one "aha" that they have with regard to the process.	The purpose of this activity is to provide students with an opportunity to tell you informally what they know and what they need help on. You can address the questions to the whole class the next day if it seems to be a common question or misunderstanding, or individually if it is something that concerns one student.

LESSON 4.6: SOLVING QUADRATICS

Length: Five class periods

Unit Sequence	Teacher Reflections
Concepts M2, C3, C4, C5	
Principles P8	
Standards SD5, SD9, SD12	
Skills S6, S8, S10, S11, S16, S17, S19, S23, S25	
Guiding Questions 1. How does the study of mathematics lend itself to explaining the world around us? 2. Why do we solve quadratic equations? 3. How do you determine which situation lends itself to a particular method for solving the quadratic? 4. What patterns exist in quadratic equations that will help us to solve them?	This lesson is being taught through the Core Curriculum parallel. Allowing students to work to develop a deep understanding of one topic will allow the students a lens through which to look as they evaluate other methods for solving quadratic equations.
Introduction, and Teaching and Learning Experiences *Expert Groups* In this activity, students will be placed in jigsaw groups in which each will become an expert in a strategy for solving quadratic equations. Once students have effectively understood the strategy, they will use a jigsaw protocol for teaching this strategy to a student in a different group. Distribute the **Expert Group Task Cards (Resources 4.14: Expert Group Task Card: Solving Quadratic Equations by Factoring, 4.15: Expert Group Task Card: Solving Quadratic Equations Using Square Roots, 4.16: Expert Group Task Card: Solving Quadratic Equations Using the Quadratic Formula, 4.17: Expert Group Task Card: Solving Quadratic Equations by Completing the Square**, and **4.18: Expert Group Task Card: Teaching Task)** that identify the various methods for solving quadratic equations that students will research. Discuss the goal for each group's assignment by reading through each task card with the group.	Students should be grouped based on their learning styles, prior knowledge, and manageability of groups you can facilitate. There are four different methods for solving equations that students will be grouped around. If students struggle with any skills related to each method, provide mini-workshops to provide assistance. It is assumed that students have learned to factor polynomials in a previous unit, so they will be focusing on how to determine if an equation is factorable, and then applying the zero product property to find the solutions to the function. Students who are assigned this method will not yet necessarily know how to complete the square, so a derivation of the quadratic formula will have to take a very

Unit Sequence	Teacher Reflections

Group 1: Solving by Factoring Expert
 	
This group will need several resources to complete this task. These materials can come from the Internet, textbook (which is the easiest option for teachers: most textbooks address each type of solving quadratic equations in its own section), mathematics teaching journal articles, books, and resource manuals. These resources should include materials that discuss
 	
1. the zero product property,
 	
2. solving quadratic equations that are equal to zero, and
 	
3. factoring polynomials:
  • factoring polynomials by removing the greatest common factor (GCF),
  • factoring trinomials into binomials, and
  • special polynomials:
    ○ the difference of two squares, and
    ○ perfect square polynomials.
 	
Solutions to Five Problems (Resource 4.14)
 	
1. $(-6, 1)$
 	
2. $(3, -5)$
 	
3. $(-2, -5)$
 	
4. $(-7, 3)$
 	
5. $(7, 4)$
	informal look so that students can see why it works. (Students are not required to perform all of the computations by themselves.)

Group 2: Solving Using the Quadratic Formula Expert This group will need several resources to complete this task. These materials can come from the Internet, textbook (which is the easiest option for teachers: most textbooks address each type of solving quadratic equations in its own section), mathematics teaching journal articles, books, and resource manuals. These resources should include materials that discuss • what the quadratic formula is, • where the quadratic formula came from, and • examples of problems that are solved using this method. A potential point for lesson extension or Ascending Intellectual Demand (AID) in this task group is to require students to understand the derivation of the quadratic formula. This is a high-level task; it requires the students to connect many different types of mathematical thinking.	Solving by using the quadratic formula has the most options for extensions. Because of this, this method should be given to those students that you believe need a more challenging assignment.

Unit Sequence	Teacher Reflections
Solutions to Five Problems (Resource 4.15: Expert Group Task Card: Solving Quadratic Equations Using the Quadratic Formula) 1. $(-3, -7)$ 2. $(6, -1.5)$ 3. $(.952, -.952)$ 4. $(1.045, -2.188)$ 5. $(2.747, -1.747)$ *Group 3: Solving Using Square Roots Expert* This group will need several resources to complete this task. These materials can come from the Internet, textbook (which is the easiest option for teachers: most textbooks address each type of solving quadratic equations in its own section), mathematics teaching journal articles, books, and resource manuals. These resources should include materials that discuss • irrational numbers, • the positive and negative values of square roots, and • how the positive and negative square roots create two solutions to the equation. **Solutions to Five Problems (Resource 4.16: Expert Group Task Card: Solving Quadratic Equations Using Square Roots)** 1. $(9.539, -9.539)$ 2. $(9.381, -9.3881)$ 3. $(5, -5)$ 4. $(10, -10)$ 5. $(7, -7)$ *Group 4: Solving by Completing the Square* This group will need several resources to complete this task. These materials can come from the Internet, textbook (which is the easiest option for teachers: most textbooks address each type of solving quadratic equations in its own section), mathematics teaching journal articles, books, and resource manuals. These resources should include materials that discuss • a review of how to complete the square, • a description of how to use completing the square to solve an equation, and • examples of how to solve quadratic equations using completing the square.	This should not just be a simple look at solving equations involving square roots. Students will be able to look at problems in depth. This means that students are looking at problems other than $x^2 = 25$. Because there are so many hands-on or visual proofs for completing the square, this might be a good group in which to place students who tend to be tactile or visual learners. Each group will need access to a computer and Internet hookup, an algebra textbook, and other books and resources that have descriptions of solving quadratics using the method that students have been assigned. Continuous discussions with the groups will help prevent students from developing misconceptions. Using questions that prompt students' reflections on their thinking process forces students to understand the "Why" and not just the "How."

Unit Sequence	Teacher Reflections
Solutions to the Five Problems (Resource 4.17: Expert Group Task Card: Solving Quadratic Equations by Completing the Square) 1. $(11, 3)$ 2. $(-5, -15)$ 3. $(94.571, -2.571)$ 4. $(4, -2)$ 5. $(5, -1)$ Once students have been assigned to a jigsaw group, they should be allowed to research how to solve a quadratic equation using their assigned method. Encourage students to ask questions to support their understanding. While students are in their groups working, you should walk around the classroom to monitor how students are constructing the understanding of the method and to address group questions. Questions to consider using while working with the groups include these: 1. Why are you approaching your problem in this manner? 2. What do you think your resource meant by that? 3. Why would you do that? 4. Can you think of an easier way to think through that idea? *Preparation for Teaching* Once a group demonstrates that all students understand why and how their method works, ask them to begin their preparation for teaching their particular method to students in the other groups. Ask students to create a teaching plan that discusses how they will instruct other students about their method for solving quadratic equations. Upon completion, students are to submit their plans for your approval prior to their instruction. The lesson plan should include these four elements: 1. Goals and objectives for their lesson 2. Informal lesson plan 3. Practice problems 4. Assessment plan	Some groups will understand their methods sooner than others, so be prepared with extension questions or scenarios that will force students to look deeper into their understanding. For example, students can investigate the derivation for the quadratic formula mentioned earlier.

Unit Sequence	Teacher Reflections
Once all group members understand their method and have their lessons approved, students are prepared to teach that method to someone else. You will then reorder the groups so that every group has a representative from each method for solving quadratic equations. Over a two-day period, the groups will need to present to each other how to solve a quadratic equation using the method in which they specialized and respond to these questions in their math journals: 1. How does the study of mathematics lend itself to explaining the world around us? 2. Why do we solve quadratic equations? 3. How do you determine which situation lends itself to a particular method for solving the quadratic equation? 4. What patterns exist in quadratic equations that will help us solve them?	By having students review these criteria with you before they teach, you are guaranteeing that students are prepared to instruct the students to whom they are assigned. This review also will give you an idea of the methods and materials students will use to guide their instruction. If possible, it is better to make sure that each group has only one member from each method group. This will create accountability for the presenters as well, and eliminate boredom and distraction within the groups. I would recommend teaming any student who is less confident or struggles academically with another team member to create this lesson plan. If you have a student who is absent on the teaching day or who absolutely cannot handle presenting in a group, you can ask that student to complete one of the following tasks: 1. Write a letter to a student who was absent describing how to solve a quadratic equation using the method to which you were assigned. This letter needs to be detailed and sequenced in a manner that makes clear how the method works. 2. Make a video of yourself teaching the assigned lesson that you could use to show a student who has missed the instructional lesson. Both tasks provide options for students who are absent during the teaching of the lessons or for students who require additional assistance in understanding how to solve quadratics. *Ascending Intellectual Demand* For each expert group, a quadratic inequality problem could be created. As the students work in their expert groups to figure out how to solve quadratic equations using the assigned method, observe their progress: if a particular group is mastering the method more quickly than other groups, provide that group with the quadratic inequality and ask those students to discuss how solving an inequality would look different using their method. Some focusing questions to help the students in their work are identified below.

Unit Sequence	Teacher Reflections
	Focusing Questions 1. What would the solution to your inequality look like on a quadratic graph? 2. When working with inequalities, we've noticed that algebraic manipulation—specifically multiplication and division—affect the inequality sign. How will that affect your solution method? 3. What additional thoughts or steps might need to be considered as you work with these inequalities?
Closure At the end of the group teaching, distribute **Resource 4.19: 3–2–1 Exit Slip Worksheet: Quadratic Equations**, allow students time to complete the worksheets, and collect individual student responses as they depart the classroom: • List **3** things you do not understand about the methods for solving quadratic equations. • List **2** ideas you need clarification on regarding these methods. • List **1** question that you still have regarding your understanding of these methods. *Homework* Ask students to complete the practice problems that their peer instructors provided them with during their instruction on each of the four methods for solving quadratic equations. Then ask students to share their problems with their peer instructors; those instructors will review the homework and clarify any misunderstanding students may have formed from their homework assignments and the responses gathered from the exit slip worksheets.	The exit slip allows you the opportunity to regroup the students for instruction based on the questions asked and the topics students list as needing clarification. *Teacher Note.* Once students have done the jigsaw activity and been exposed to these ideas or methods, they may need more time to practice what they have learned; for that reason, it may be necessary to build in more practice time.

LESSON 4.7: SOLVING QUADRATICS ASSESSMENT

Length: Two half-day class periods

Unit Sequence	Teacher Reflections
Concepts M3, C3, C4, C5	
Principles P8	
Standards SD5, SD7, SD9, SD10	
Skills S15, S16, S19, S23, S25	
Introduction, and Teaching and Learning Experiences *First Half-Day Session* Distribute **Resource 4.20: Solving Quadratic Equations Mini-Project Choices** to the students. Discuss the fact that there are three choices from which to select; based on their learning preferences, students might be drawn to one project more than to the others. Ask them to read through these task options and to generate questions that may help them get started with the assignment. **Mini-Project Options** • *Practical Task.* Your task is to create a problem that you would solve using each method for solving quadratic equations that you just learned. Explain how to solve that problem. • *Analytical Task.* Your task is to create a "Dummies Guide" for solving quadratic equations. Highlight each type of solution, explain how to solve it, and explain under which conditions it is the best solution to use. • *Creative Task.* Your task is to create a game that involves using each type of solving quadratics as a benchmark for winning the game. These projects will take about a week for students to work on and refine.	This assessment addresses the Curriculum of Connections parallel by allowing students to make connections between what they have been learning through their research on other ideas outside the mathematical classroom. By allowing students to select a project designed around thinking preferences, I knew that I could assess how my students like to think and learn; this assessment provides me with some understanding about their personal identities as mathematicians. The purpose behind this assessment is to give students the opportunity to show that they have mastered the ideas and concepts behind solving quadratic equations. So often, students are asked to just regurgitate formulas and never show a true understanding of what it is that is going on behind the numbers and variables that they are manipulating. These mini-projects are designed so that students can show mastery while looking at the process through a lens that supports the manner in which they think.

Unit Sequence	Teacher Reflections
Second Half-Day Session Allow students the opportunity to show their projects to their peers and receive feedback that assists them in making necessary or suggested changes if they feel it brings depth and broader understanding of the topics they address in their projects.	The purpose behind this second half-day session is to create a learning situation wherein students refine their project to communicate their understanding of the solving of quadratic equations. Students will often submit a much more refined final project if they are given the opportunity for feedback along the way. This is a skill we use as adults daily, and I want my students to use feedback as an invaluable tool. Allowing students to look at another's work through the lens of a mathematics student and a mathematician encourages them to use the Curriculum of Identity parallel to shape their work and understanding as well as those with whom they are working.
Closure Ask students to turn in their mini-projects for further assessment using **Resource 4.21: Quadratics Mini-Project Rubric**, which will guide your evaluation.	

LESSON 4.8: DISCRIMINANT . . . I THOUGHT IT WAS A BAD THING?

Length: One class period

Unit Sequence	Teacher Reflections
Concepts M2, C2	
Principles P10	
Standards SD7, SD8, SD12, SD13	
Skills S5, S6, S8, S12, S18, S21	
Guiding Questions 1. How does the discriminant help us solve quadratic functions? 2. What is the relationship between the zeros in the graphs of quadratic functions and the value of the discriminant?	Students will need the following resources for this lesson: handout, graphing calculators (at minimum one per group; one per student would be ideal).
Introduction, and Teaching and Learning Experiences *Opening Up the Discussion* In a class discussion, show the students the quadratic formula. Explain to them that the part of the formula that is under the radical sign is called the "discriminant." Work with the students to evaluate the discriminant for the following quadratic function: $$2x^2 + 3x + 3 = 0$$ The discriminant $= -15$ because $$\begin{aligned} b^2 - 4ac &= 3^2 - 4(2)(3) \\ &= 9 - 8(3) \\ &= 9 - 24 \\ &= -15 \end{aligned}$$ Now inform the students that they are going to do some work with their partners to determine if the discriminant can help us to solve quadratic equations (use **Resource 4.22: The Discriminant, and Solutions to Quadratic Functions**).	This lesson is being taught using the Curriculum of Connections parallel. Students are being asked to use their knowledge of quadratic graphs to help them determine the relationship between the discriminant and the number of zeros that a function has. Using graphing calculators in this lesson will allow students to quickly see the relationship between the number of solutions and the value of the discriminant. If students have not had a lot of graphing calculator experience, they may

Unit Sequence	Teacher Reflections
Assign students in pairs that represent similar learning styles. Have students work with their partner to graph the following functions on their calculators and to copy their graphs onto the graph paper provided on the sheet.	need a refresher on these procedures using the graphing calculator. You do not want the technology to get in the way of the lesson. The refresher should focus on the following skills:

$$x^2 + 2x + 3 = 0$$
$$x^2 - 2x + 1 = 0$$
$$x^2 - 2x - 2 = 0$$
$$2x^2 + 3x + 3 = 0$$
$$x^2 - 2x + 4 = 0$$
$$3x^2 - 6x + 3 = 0$$
$$x^2 + 6x + 10 = 0$$
$$3x^2 - 18x = -27$$
$$-5x^2 - 10x = 0$$
$$-x^2 = 4x + 6$$

- How to enter a function into the calculator
- How to adjust the window setting so that students can see the whole function
- How to use the trace function so that they may find the values of the zeros of their function quickly

In addition to copying, have the students identify the zeros of each function, then have students work to evaluate the discriminant of each function.

Once students have completed the work, ask them look for a relationship between the discriminant and solutions to the functions. After the partners have had a chance to complete the assignment and identify a relationship, discuss as a whole class what patterns the students notice, making sure to hit on the following ideas:

- If the discriminant is positive, there are two real solutions to the function.
- If the discriminant is negative, there are no real solutions to the function.
- If the discriminant is zero, there is one real solution to the function.

Students may get caught up on the value of the zeros in their functions. If this occurs, have students add a column to their worksheet that identifies the actual number of zeros each function has.

Closure

Have each student complete the exit ticket, **Resource 4.23: Exit Slip Worksheet,** prior to leaving the class. This worksheet asks students to discuss the following questions:

1. What relationship exists between the value of the discriminant and the number of solutions that a quadratic relationship has? (Be specific in your response.)

2. How can you use the discriminant to help you solve quadratic functions?

The assessment for this activity is to have students complete an exit slip. The exit slip will simply ask two questions. Based on the answers, you will be able to follow up individually with students who still struggle with these ideas.

LESSON 4.9: FLIGHT OF A ROCKET

Length: Three class periods (one period to build the rockets, one period to launch the rockets, and one period to analyze the rocket flight and report findings)

Unit Sequence	Teacher Reflections
Concepts M1, C2	
Principles P2, P3, P5, P6	
Standards SD2, SD3, SD5, SD7, SD10, SD11, SD13	
Skills S2, S3, S4, S6, S9, S12, S13, S15, S21	
Guiding Questions 1. What in the world around me is quadratic? 2. How do I use quadratic relationships to model the world around me? 3. How can technology allow me to see the world around me mathematically?	This lesson is being taught through the Curriculum of Practice parallel. It assists students to observe and analyze a quadratic activity as it happens outside the classroom, determine the usefulness and inner workings of different quadratic relationships, and reinforce the importance and value of these concepts within a contextual setting.

Introduction, and Teaching and Learning Experiences
 	
Rocket Building
 	
Distribute rocket-building kits to students who have been arranged in four-member teams. Tell students that as they construct their rockets they can adapt the design plans based on consensus of their group members.
   Distribute the **Resource 4.24: Flight of a Rocket** worksheet to discuss with students the data that they will gather during the actual launch. On the day that students fly their rockets, the groups will have to designate responsibilities in order to gather the proper data for their activity:
 	
• *Timer.* Responsible for timing the flight of the rocket from takeoff to landing
• *Videographer.* Responsible for videotaping the flight from beginning to end, making sure that the flight path of the rocket and the benchmarks are clearly visible in the video so that it can be used for analysis later
	Materials Needed
	
	• Video camera
	• Rocket-building kit
	• Rocket launch pad
	• Outdoor location where rocket launch can take place and landmarks can be used as a means to measure the max point, zeros, and so on
	
	Grouping
	
	Group students by readiness levels (mixed or homogeneous) or by learning style, depending on the nature of your students and the rocket resources you have available.
	   Students should record their rocket design in their math journals so they can look back on the building process when they present their final equation.
	   There are many different types of rocket kits and launch pads that students can use for this project. Depending on cost and extent of time that will be spent building these rockets, you can decide on what type of rockets students can use.

Unit Sequence	Teacher Reflections

• *Rocket coordinator.* Responsible for rocket from beginning of launch through recovery
• *Launch controller.* Responsible for actual launch of rocket and coordinating all of the other team members so that they are aware of the start of the launch and are able to fulfill their responsibilities
 	
Analyzing the Video Launch
 	
After students have built their rockets and collected their launch data, they will need to spend time analyzing their launch video. Students will need to download the videos of their rocket flights and use the information that they can gather from their video to write an equation that represents the height of their rocket's flight over time.
   Once the students have written an equation, have them check the equation against the data that they collected to make sure that the equation predicts at least five points (*time, height*) accurately on their video.
   Next, students will need to create a graph and a table using their equation that represents the flight of their rocket.
   Have students label different points on the graph that correlate with events during their launch. There should be at least three points labeled on the graph (*x*-intercept, *y*-intercept, and the vertex) but other points are welcomed.
 	
Final Presentations
 	
Finally, ask the students to prepare a quick presentation of what they did to write their equations and share their graphs and tables with the rest of the class, as well as any problems or struggles that they encountered.
	Water and air rockets both are easy to build from materials easily found at home; these do not fly very high, though, making it difficult for the students to measure their rocket's flight path. The directions for making both types of rockets can easily be found on the Internet or as a part of many science curriculums. For a little more money, you can purchase complete rocket kits from a local or online hobby shop. This activity is also a great opportunity to reach out to your colleagues in the science department and work on cross-curricular activities.
	   Once students are ready to launch the rockets, it is important to find a launch space where you can launch the rocket but also have a benchmark to use for the height of the rocket's flight. If possible, find a place next to a wall, where you can mark the different heights or at least know the measurements of the wall so that students can use that information as they analyze their video. This method of measuring height will work best with water or air rockets. If you go with more-detailed rockets that achieve higher flight, then you will need to look into alternative methods for measuring height or at least alternative methods to determine the height of the benchmarks that are used, because it becomes increasingly difficult to measure the higher heights without more-sophisticated tools.
	   Guiding questions to ask the students as they work on their equations include these:
	
	• Can you identify the vertex/maximum value to the nearest 100th of a second?
	• What are the zeros of the function?
	• Are there any other details from the rocket launch that would be helpful?
	• Can you make a table of time and height?
	
	Alternative Culminating Activity for Rocket Lesson
	
	Have the students edit their videos to show what they thought were the important or fun parts of the activity. At the end of the video, students should input a still frame that shows the equation they wrote to represent the flight path of their rocket. You can then put all the edited videos together so that they run in a loop. The video can be shown to the whole class as a documentary of their journey through this lesson. The video could then be highlighted in a showcase or display area in the school building

Unit Sequence	Teacher Reflections
	where it plays on a loop, and where there are examples of the rockets that were made and the work that students submitted for the project. If there is no area in the building where student work can be showcased, this video could be used as part of a portfolio night where you invite parents to come to the school to look at the work students have done over the course of the year, semester, or unit.

Closure
 	
Have students hang their graphs and tables around the classroom.
  Discuss the similarities and differences in the graphs, tables, and equations that students created.
  Students need to record their final graphs, tables, and equations into their math journals, along with a reflection of the process that they went through. They also will respond to the following questions:
 	
1. What in the world around me is quadratic?
 	
2. How do I use quadratic relationships to model the world around me?
 	
3. How can technology allow me to see the world around me mathematically?
	This discussion time allows you to point out similarities of y-intercepts, x-intercepts, and differences in the equation forms that students used, as well as processes that were followed.

LESSON 4.10: UNIT CLOSURE

Length: One class period

Unit Sequence	Teacher Reflections
Introduction, and Teaching and Learning Experiences *How Far Have You Come?* As a means to bring closure to the end of the unit, ask students to bring their mathematical learning journals to class; return their pre-assessments to them. Ask students to go back through their pre-assessments and look at the problems that they solved with the purpose of identifying the problems in which they have seen most progress in understanding since the beginning of the unit. (Students should look through the problems and renumber the level of difficulty of each problem from 1 to 5, as they did in the pre-assessment.) Once students have identified their growth in understanding, ask them to find the pages in their mathematical learning journals that show the work they have completed to reinforce that understanding. This activity will take about 30 minutes. Once the students have been able to document places where they have gained new knowledge and understanding, ask them to go back to their learning style groups that were designated in Lesson 4.1. In these groups, students will break into smaller groups of three or four and discuss the learning that they experienced during this unit. Specifically, the students need to focus on what topics they showed growth in and which lessons were most helpful in helping them gain this knowledge. Ask them if they noticed as they worked with their peers which ones have similar and varying learning styles and about the type of instruction that supports their understanding of mathematics. The following questions can be used to guide their reflections in the group:	This culminating lesson is used to have students self-assess their progress in mathematics and discuss their personal style preference, which can influence their understanding of mathematical concepts. As students work on their self-analysis and group analyses, you should move around the room to observe and record and assess students' reflections. This is an opportunity for you to listen to how each student has been shaped by the major concepts, knowledge, and skills that are the focus of the unit. Additionally, this session provides you with the opportunity to build self-efficacy in young people by allowing each student to share his personal views of his own academic and personal growth.

Unit Sequence	Teacher Reflections

Group Focusing Questions
 	
 • In what areas or topics in this unit did you show the most growth?
 • Was there a particular topic that you understand better?
 • What lessons or activities brought you the most understanding?
 • As a learning style group, are you noticing any particular lessons or activities that helped the group as a whole?
 • Is there a concept where you did not see growth?
   o What is it about the concept where you did not see growth that you feel is creating your struggle?
   o How are you going to gain understanding of this concept now that we are at the end of this unit of study?
	Ask students to turn in these reflections and their journals at the end of this session. The responses will provide a way for you to assess individual growth and to provide ongoing academic assistance to students.

SUGGESTED READING

Scieszka, J. (1995). *Math curse*. New York: Penquin Books.

RESOURCES

The following Resources can be found at the companion website for *Parallel Curriculum Units for Mathematics, Grades 6–12* at www.corwin.com/math6–12.

RESOURCE 4.1

Math Learning Styles Worksheet

Name: _____ Date: _____ Period: _____

❏ Read the definitions below.

❏ Determine which definition best matches how you like to learn math most of the time. You may come across more than one definition that fits your learning style; if that is the case, you should choose the style that you use most often.

❏ Please respond to the statements on the back of the page.

1. "When I solve a math problem, I like to work step by step."

2. "When I solve a math problem, I like to look for patterns, categorize things, or find reasons for why my solution(s) works."

3. "When I solve a math problem, I like to talk with other people about the problem or connect it to something I've done before."

4. "When I solve a math problem, I tend to picture the problem in my head or create an image of the problem. I also tend to try many different strategies until I find the one that works."

My Learning Style is _____.

- If you chose **1** you are a *Mastery Style* learner.
- If you chose **2** you are an *Understanding Style* learner.
- If you chose **3** you are an *Interpersonal Style* learner.
- If you chose **4** you are a *Self-Expressive Style* learner.

❏ Answer the following questions. As you answer them, think back to all of the math classes you have had during your student career.

1. What really helps you learn math? (Another way to think of this is, How do you learn math best?)

2. What is the least helpful when you are learning math? (Another way to think of this is, What situations get in the way of your math learning?)

RESOURCE 4.2

Flight of a Ball: Group Activity

Name: _____ Date: _____ Period: _____

❏ Read the directions.

❏ In your group, continue to discuss the flight and characteristics of the ball toss.

❏ As a group, create a table that represents the height of the ball over time. (There are additional tennis balls in the front of the room if you need them.)

❏ Use the table you created to construct a graph that represents the height of the ball over time.

❏ Have your table and graph approved by me.

❏ Re-create your table and graph on large butcher paper.

Table	Graph

RESOURCE 4.3

Flight of a Ball: Reflections

Name: _____ Date: _____ Period: _____

☐ Read the directions.
☐ Once your butcher paper graphs and tables have been created, answer Questions 1–6 as a group. Make sure to record the answers on the sheet.

1. How did you know where to start your table?

2. Why did you choose the time intervals you chose?

3. What does the data on the graph and table reveal?

4. What was the graph's maximum height?

5. Does this graph cross the x-axis?

    Where, and what does this reveal to you?

6. Does the graph cross the y-axis?

    Where, and what does this reveal to you?

RESOURCE 4.4

Flight of a Ball: Post-Class Discussion

☐ After the class has discussed the different tables and graphs each group has made, answer the following questions in your group.

1. How are the graph and table of the height of the ball over time related?

2. Which parts of the graph and table show you where the ball starts, stops, and reaches its highest point?

3. Which form—the graph or the table—do you find easier to use?

☐ Record the following items in your mathematical learning journal:

- A copy of the table and the graph.
- Identify on the sketches where the graph and table indicate the start and stop of the ball, and the maximum height.
- Record the mathematical vocabulary words that explain where the ball stops and starts, and the maximum height.
- Describe the situation your group created where the graph and table would have a minimum point.
- How is the change you have seen in the flight of the ball alike or different from other mathematical relationships (e.g., linear, exponential) you have worked with this year?

RESOURCE 4.5

Homework Slip

Name: _____ Date: _____ Period: _____

☐ Read the directions.
☐ Find a parabola somewhere in your surroundings.
☐ Take a picture of this parabola with a digital camera or camera phone.
☐ If a camera is not available, draw a picture of that parabola.
☐ Be sure to bring your digital file or picture to class tomorrow.

- -

Homework Slip

Name: _____ Date: _____ Period: _____

☐ Read the directions.
☐ Find a parabola somewhere in your surroundings.
☐ Take a picture of this parabola with a digital camera or camera phone.
☐ If a camera is not available, draw a picture of that parabola.
☐ Be sure to bring your digital file or picture to class tomorrow.

- -

Homework Slip

Name: _____ Date: _____ Period: _____

☐ Read the directions.
☐ Find a parabola somewhere in your surroundings.
☐ Take a picture of this parabola with a digital camera or camera phone.
☐ If a camera is not available, draw a picture of that parabola.
☐ Be sure to bring your digital file or picture to class tomorrow.

RESOURCE 4.6

Paper-and-Pencil Pre-Assessment, Part I

Name: _____ Date: _____ Period: _____

☐ Read the directions.
☐ Show all work when possible.
☐ If you don't know how to do a problem, skip it. This is a pre-assessment and it is expected that there will be things that you do not know how to do yet.
☐ As you solve each problem, list your comfort level (1 to 5) in the box next to the problem.

1 = I've never done this type of problem before.

3 = I've seen this before, but I'm not sure I'm doing it correctly.

5 = This is the easiest problem I've ever solved.

1. Use the equation $y = -2 \times 2 + 4$ to complete the following tasks.

    a. Make a table that represents the function.

    b. Create a graph of the function using the grid that follows.

    c. On this graph, please label the following things:

       Max/min points

       Vertex

       Axis of symmetry

       Zeros

       y-intercept

RESOURCE 4.7

Responding to Essential Understanding
Pre-Assessment, Part II

Name: _____ Date: _____ Period: _____

❑ Read the directions.

❑ Answer the following questions. These are opinion questions, so be detailed and support your opinion.

❑ If possible, use a mathematical example to support your thinking.

❑ Later, you will add these answers to your math journal.

1. How does the way in which something changes predict its true form? (This can also be thought of as, How do the number patterns indicate the type of function you are working with?)

2. How are mathematical patterns communicated through

situations?

equations?

graphs?

tables?

3. Is math a language? If so, how is it used as a descriptor of your world?

4. How are graphs and tables related?

RESOURCE 4.8

Creating the Coordinate Grid

Name: _____ Date: _____ Period: _____

The purpose of this assignment is to take the parabola that you found outside math class and represent it on a four-quadrant graph as it might be seen in an analytical report or mathematics textbook.

❑ Obtain a copy of your real-world parabola.

❑ Use your copy and what you know about the parabola that you found in the real world to place that parabola on a four-quadrant graph.

❑ Make sure that the data points on your graph correspond with the points that you saw in your parabola in its original environment.

❑ If possible, label the x- and y-axes.

❑ Be sure to indicate the x and y scale of the graph.

❑ Title your graph so that we know what the parabola is supposed to represent.

❑ Once you've created the graph, please label the following items:

Vertex

Max/min value

Axis of symmetry

x-intercepts

y-intercept

❑ Below, describe what each of the points that you labeled above tells you about your graph.

❑ Vertex _____

❑ Max/min value _____

❑ Axis of symmetry _____

❑ x-intercepts _____

❑ y-intercept _____

RESOURCE 4.9

The Parabola Curse: Homework Assignment

Name: _____ Date: _____ Period: _____

❑ Answer the questions below based on your experiences in class over the past few days.

❑ Be sure to use complete sentences and restate the question in your answer.

❑ This assignment is due _____.

1. What about parabolas makes them occur naturally in our surroundings?

2. Why do human beings look for ways to understand the world around them?

3. How does the study of mathematics lend itself to explaining the world around us?

4. What about projectile motion makes it mathematical?

5. How can quadratic relationships be used to describe the change in a projectile's height?

RESOURCE 4.10

Figurate Numbers Task Card: Triangular Numbers

Given the figurate numbers below, complete the following tasks.

Shape 1   Shape 2   Shape 3

1. Draw Figures 0, 4, and 5 based on Figures 1, 2, and 3 that you were given.

2. Make a table of the figure number, n, and the total number of dots in that number, t, for Shapes 0 to 5.

3. Use the figures to write an expression that relates the figure number, n, to the total number of dots in the shape, t.

4. Use your equation to predict the number of dots in Shape 100.

5. Create a written description or guide to seeing the pattern in your shape that inspired your equation.

RESOURCE 4.11

Figurate Numbers Task Card: Square Numbers

Given the figurate numbers below, complete the following tasks.

Shape 1　　　　Shape 2　　　　Shape 3

1. Draw Figures 0, 4, and 5 based on Figures 1, 2, and 3 that you were given.

2. Make a table of the figure number, n, and the total number of dots in that number, t, for Shapes 0 to 5.

3. Use the figures to write an expression that relates the figure number, n, to the total number of dots in the shape, t.

4. Use your equation to predict the number of dots in Shape 100.

5. Create a written description or guide to seeing the pattern in your shape that inspired your equation.

RESOURCE 4.12

Figurate Numbers Task Card: Rectangular Numbers

Given the figurate numbers below, complete the following tasks.

Shape 1　　　　Shape 2　　　　Shape 3

1. Draw Figures 0, 4, and 5 based on Figures 1, 2, and 3 that you were given.

2. Make a table of the figure number, n, and the total number of dots in that number, t, for Shapes 0 to 5.

3. Use the figures to write an expression that relates the figure number, n, to the total number of dots in the shape, t.

4. Use your equation to predict the number of dots in Shape 100.

5. Create a written description or guide to seeing the pattern in your shape that inspired your equation.

RESOURCE 4.13

3–2–1 Exit Slip Worksheet

Name: _____ Date: _____ Period: _____

List **3** things you understand about the methods for writing equations for quadratic patterns.

List **2** ideas you need clarification on in regards to identifying and writing equations for quadratic patterns.

List **1** question or an "aha" that you have regarding your understanding of writing equations to represent quadratic patterns.

RESOURCE 4.14

Expert Group Task Card:
Solving Quadratic Equations by Factoring

Name: _____ Date: _____ Period: _____

❏ In your groups, review the materials I have provided to you about solving quadratic equations by factoring.

❏ Use what you have done to solve the five problems at the bottom of this sheet.

❏ Based on what you have read and the work you did to solve the five problems, answer the questions below. This work should be copied and stored in your math journal.

1. What are the important ideas that you should have taken from these materials?

2. Briefly describe what you are doing when you solve a quadratic equation by factoring.

3. What types of equations do you feel this method should be used with?

4. Are there any clues or identifying traits that will let you know when to use this method to solve quadratic equations?

5. As a group, create a step-by-step guide or discussion that you can use to explain this method to students who are not part of your expert group. As part of this guide, create five practice problems that you can use in your instruction.

RESOURCE 4.15

**Expert Group Task Card: Solving Quadratic Equations
Using the Quadratic Formula**

Name: _____ Date: _____ Period: _____

❐ In your groups, review the materials I have provided about solving quadratic equations by using the quadratic formula.

❐ Use what you have done to solve the five problems at the bottom of this sheet.

❐ Based on what you have read and the work you did to solve the five problems, answer the questions below.

❐ This work should be copied and stored in your math journal.

1. What are the important ideas that you should have taken from these materials?

2. Briefly describe what you are doing when you solve a quadratic equation by factoring.

3. What types of equations do you feel this method should be used with?

4. Are there any clues or identifying traits that will let you know when to use this method to solve quadratic equations?

5. Describe where the quadratic equation came from.

RESOURCE 4.16

**Expert Group Task Card: Solving Quadratic Equations
Using Square Roots**

Name: _____ Date: _____ Period: _____

❐ In your groups, review the materials I have provided to you about solving quadratic equations using square roots.

❐ Use what you have done to solve the five problems at the bottom of this sheet.

❐ Based on what you have read and the work you did to solve the five problems, answer the questions below.

❐ This work should be copied or stored in your math journal.

1. What are the important ideas that you should have taken from these materials?

2. Briefly describe what you are doing when you solve a quadratic equation with square roots.

3. What types of equations do you feel this method should be used with?

4. Are there any clues or identifying traits that will let you know when to use this method to solve quadratic equations?

5. As a group, create a step-by-step guide or discussion that you can use to explain this method to students who are not part of your expert group. As part of this guide, create five practice problems that you can use in your instruction.

RESOURCE 4.17

**Expert Group Task Card: Solving Quadratic
Equations by Completing the Square**

Name: _____ Date: _____ Period: _____

❐ In your groups, review the materials I have provided to you about solving quadratic equations by factoring.

❐ Use what you have done to solve the five problems at the bottom of this sheet.

❐ Based on what you have read and the work you did to solve the five problems, answer the questions below.

❐ This work should be copied and stored in your math journal.

1. What are the important ideas that you have taken from these materials?

2. Briefly describe what you are doing when you solve a quadratic equation by completing the square.

3. With what types of equations do you feel this method should be used?

4. Are there any clues or identifying traits that will let you know when to use this method to solve quadratic equations?

5. As a group, create a step-by-step guide or discussion that you can use to explain this method to students who are not part of your expert group. As part of this guide, create five practice problems that you can use in your instruction.

RESOURCE 4.18

Expert Group Task Card: Teaching Task

Name: _____ Date: _____ Period: _____

❐ Now that you have become an expert in your method of solving quadratic equations, you need to complete the following tasks in order to share your expertise with the other groups.

Before Your Assigned Teaching Day . . .

• Create a lesson plan to use while teaching your method to the other groups.
• Your lesson plan should include
  ○ objectives that you want your students to meet,
  ○ guided notes that your students can use to follow your instruction and examples,
  ○ practice problems for your students,
  ○ five homework problems for your students to use as practice,
  ○ an answer key to your practice problems, and
  ○ an answer key to your homework problems.
• Submit your lesson plan to your teacher for final approval before you provide your instruction.

On Your Assigned Teaching Day . . .

• Present your lesson to your students.
• Provide your students with copies of your guided notes.
• Do your best to answer questions and clarify misunderstandings.
• Assign your homework and practice problems.

After Your Assigned Teaching Day . . .

• Review the homework and practice problems with your students and go over the answers.
• Help them understand their mistakes and answer any questions that they may have.
• Answer the following questions in your math journal:
  ○ What were the most common misunderstandings or misconceptions?
  ○ Why do you believe students misunderstood or held these misconceptions? Was it something you said or presented? What is a misunderstanding of a previous concept?
  ○ Thinking about the three other methods you learned:
    – What was the easiest method for you to understand?
    – What was the hardest method for you to understand?
    – Which method do you believe will be the most useful to you? Why?

RESOURCE 4.19

3–2–1 Exit Slip Worksheet: Quadratic Equations

Name: _____ Date: _____ Period: _____

List **3** things you understand about the methods for solving quadratic equations.

List **2** ideas you need clarification on regarding these methods.

List **1** question or an "aha" that you still have regarding your understanding of these methods.

RESOURCE 4.20

Solving Quadratic Equations Mini-Project Choices

Name: _____ Date: _____ Period: _____

Practical Task

☐ Your task is to create a problem that you would solve using each method for solving quadratic equations that you just learned. Explain how to solve that problem.

If you choose this option for your mini-project, make sure that the following things are included in your project.

- Address all four methods.
- For each problem that you create,
  - identify the method that you are using to solve the problem,
  - solve the problem,
  - explain, in paragraph format, the steps that you used to solve that problem, and
  - explain why the problem is best solved using the method you chose.

Analytical Task

☐ Your task is to create a "Dummies Guide" for solving quadratic equations. Highlight each type of solution, explain how to solve it, and explain under which conditions it is the best solution to use.

If you choose this option for your mini-project, make sure that the following steps are included in your project.

- Address all four methods.
- For each method, provide a detailed description of how to use the method. This should be written for somebody who has never used the method before.
- For each method, provide a detailed description of the types of problems or conditions where the method works best.
- Your descriptions need to be written using proper grammar and mechanics so as to guarantee accessibility to all readers who use your guide.

Creative Task

☐ Your task is to create a game that involves using each type of solving quadratics as a benchmark for winning the game.

RESOURCE 4.21

Quadratics Mini-Project Rubric

Name: _____ Date: _____ Period: _____

Advanced	Proficient	Emerging Proficient	Unsatisfactory
In addition to meeting all of the requirements of being proficient, the project involves detailed examples above the required four methods to allow for a new level of clarity and understanding of the methods. —or— Student has created a problem or example set that allows for a novice with solving quadratic equations to truly understand the purpose and use of these methods.	Complete examples of all four methods for solving quadratic equations. • Quadratic equation • Using square roots • Completing the square • Factoring Somebody who has never used these methods to solve quadratics would understand the descriptions of how to use them.	Complete examples of three of the four methods for solving quadratic equations. Somebody who has never used these methods to solve quadratics would understand most of the descriptions of how to use them.	Complete examples of two of the four methods for solving quadratic equations. —or— Incomplete examples of all four methods for solving quadratic equations. —or— The descriptions of how to use these methods are difficult to understand or create new misunderstandings.

RESOURCE 4.22

The Discriminant, and Solutions to Quadratic Functions

Name: _____ Date: _____ Period: _____

☐ Graph the functions below using the graphing calculator.
☐ Copy that graph onto this sheet.
☐ Identify the zeros for each function using the graph.
☐ Evaluate the discriminant for each function.
☐ Look for any relationships you see between the discriminant and quadratic functions.

Function	Graph	Zeros	Discriminant
$x^2 + 2x + 3 = 0$			
$x^2 - 2x + 1 = 0$			

RESOURCE 4.23

Exit Slip Worksheet

1. What relationship exists between the value of the discriminant and the number of solutions that a quadratic relationship has? (Be specific in your response.)

2. How can you use the discriminant to help you solve quadratic functions?

RESOURCE 4.24

Flight of a Rocket

After you have flown your rocket and collected your data, complete the following tasks:

❏ Write an equation that represents the height of your rocket over time.

❏ Check your equation against five points from your data.

❏ Use your equation to create a table that represents the height of your rocket over time.

❏ Use your equation and table to create a graph that represents the height of your rocket over time.

- Label the *x*-intercepts, *y*-intercept, and the vertex on your graph.
- Explain what those points mean in terms of the flight of your rocket.

❏ Place a copy of your graph, table, and explanation in your math journal.

❏ Prepare a quick three- to five-minute presentation for the class about what your equation represents. Be sure to include

- your process for finding the equation,
- any struggles you had,
- a description of what the intercepts and vertex mean in terms of the experiment, and
- a class-size copy of your table, graph, and equation.

Index

CORWIN

A SAGE Company

The Corwin logo—a raven striding across an open book—represents the union of courage and learning. Corwin is committed to improving education for all learners by publishing books and other professional development resources for those serving the field of PreK–12 education. By providing practical, hands-on materials, Corwin continues to carry out the promise of its motto: **"Helping Educators Do Their Work Better."**